Critical Thinking About
Environmental Issues

Energy

Critical Thinking About
Environmental Issues

Energy

Other books in the Critical Thinking About
Environmental Issues series are:

Endangered Species
Forest Fires
Global Warming
Pesticides

Critical Thinking About
Environmental Issues

Energy

By Jane S. Shaw and Manuel Nikel-Zueger

GREENHAVEN
PRESS®

GALE

San Diego • Detroit • New York • San Francisco • Cleveland
New Haven, Conn. • Waterville, Maine • London • Munich

LIBRARY OF CONGRESS CATALOGING-IN-PUBLICATION DATA

Shaw, Jane S., and Nikel-Zueger, Manuel.
  Energy / By Jane S. Shaw and Manuel Nikel-Zueger.
    p. cm. — (Critical thinking about environmental issues)
Summary: Discusses controversies surrounding energy such as whether we are running out of energy, energy development on public lands, the harmfulness of current energy sources, alternatives to fossil fuel, the government influence on energy use, and future concerns.
Includes bibliographical references and index.
  ISBN 0-7377-1268-6
  [1. Power resources. 2. Environmental protection.] I. Title. II. Critical thinking about environmental issues series.
  TJ163.2.N54 2004
  333.79—dc22

2003015734

Printed in the United States of America

Contents

Foreword

If a nation expects to be ignorant and free . . . it expects
what never was and never will be.

Thomas Jefferson

Thomas Jefferson understood that a free nation depends on
an educated citizenry. Citizens must have the level of
knowledge necessary to make informed decisions on complex public policy issues. In the United States, schools have a major responsibility for developing that knowledge.

In the twenty-first century, American citizens will struggle with
environmental questions of the first order. These include complicated and contentious topics such as global warming, pesticide use,
and species extinction. The goal of this series, Critical Thinking
About Environmental Issues, is to help young people recognize
the complexity of these topics and help them view the issues an-
alytically and objectively.

All too often, environmental problems are treated as moral issues. For example, using pesticides is often considered bad because
residues may be found on food and because the application of pesticides may harm birds. In contrast, relying on organic food (produced without insecticides or herbicides) is considered good. Yet
this simplistic approach fails to recognize the role of pesticides in
producing food for the world and ignores the scientific studies that
suggest that pesticides cause little harm to humans. Such superfi-
cial treatment of multifaceted issues does not serve citizens well
and provides a poor basis for education.

This series, Critical Thinking About Environmental Issues, ex-
poses students to the complexities of each issue it addresses. While
the books touch on many aspects of each environmental problem,
their goal is primarily to point out the differences in scientific
opinion surrounding the topics. These books present the facts that
underlie different scientific interpretations. They also address dif-
fering values that may affect the interpretation of the facts and economic questions that may affect policy choices.

The goal of the series is to open up inquiry on issues that are
often viewed too narrowly. Each book, written in language that is

understandable to young readers, provides enough information about the scientific theories and methods for the reader to weigh the merits of the leading arguments. Ultimately, students, like adult citizens, will make their own decisions.

With environmental issues, especially those where new science is always emerging, the possibility exists that there is not enough information to settle the issue. If this is the case, the books may spur readers to pursue the topics further. If readers come away from this series critically examining their own opinions as well as others' and eager to seek more information, the goal of these books will have been achieved.

by Jane S. Shaw
Series Editor

CHAPTER 1

Are We Running Out of Energy?

New Yorkers were stunned and bewildered when they witnessed giant passenger jets speed headlong into the World Trade Center towers on September 11, 2001. The tragedy was as unexpected as it was unimaginable. Both skyscrapers collapsed, killing more than twenty-eight hundred people. Two other planes crashed, one into the Pentagon and one into a field in Pennsylvania. Americans were aghast at the first attack on their country since Pearl Harbor on December 7, 1941.

National security became an immediate issue, and citizens began to consider the ways that the United States was at risk. For the first time in many years, many began to question the nation's dependence on foreign oil. The world's largest oil reserves are located in the Middle East around the Persian Gulf, the area from which the September 11 killers had come and where anti-American sentiment is often strong. Imports of petroleum into the United States have been rising for many years and now exceed 52 percent of the nation's oil consumption. In 2001 about 23 percent of all U.S. imports came from the Persian Gulf region. As Americans looked at places where they might be vulnerable, it was natural to consider the possibility of cutoffs of oil by unfriendly countries.

Petroleum is critical to the way we live. Distilled into gasoline, petroleum powers cars and other vehicles. It also provides fuel oil for homes and factories and jet fuel for airplanes, and it is the feedstock for numerous synthetic products, from plastics in packaging and appliances to fabrics such as polyester and Gore-Tex.

True, oil is not the only fuel used in the United States. Other sources of energy are more homegrown. Homes, businesses, and plants are heated by natural gas, most of which currently comes from within the country. Air conditioning, computers, telephones, and microwaves—to name a few—are powered with electricity. Although electricity can be produced with a variety of fuels, half the electricity in the United States is produced from coal-fired power plants, and almost all coal is produced domestically. Even so, concern about overdependence on petroleum from foreign sources has permeated Americans' consciousness.

At the same time, many people are deeply anxious about protecting their environment. They fear that the price the United States must pay to become less dependent on outside sources of energy is to dig deep into its mountains and forests, polluting the air and excessively warming the earth.

Concern about overdependence on petroleum from foreign sources has permeated Americans' consciousness.

The apparent conflict between energy independence and environmental protection matters because convenient, reliable energy has become integral to people's lives. Living without it is nearly unthinkable. Since the Industrial Revolution in the eighteenth century, people have increasingly relied on machines to do work—from James Watt's steam engine, a cornerstone of the Industrial Revolution, to the electricity-powered computers that we use today. These machines need energy. From video games to robots, energy is an inextricable part of modern life.

Americans were reminded just how inextricable energy is when a giant power shortage hit the northeastern United States and parts of Canada on August 14, 2003. It was the largest blackout in the history of North America. In a matter of minutes, blackouts swept across eight states and southern Ontario, turning out lights, darkening computer screens, halting elevators, stopping clocks, and immobilizing subways. Some people were without power for nearly two days.

Interviewing those who experienced the shortages, two *Wall Street Journal* reporters discovered that many simple tasks could not be done when, in their words, "the Electronic Age blew a fuse."[1] They reported on a grocery store where the cashier had to go back to pencil and paper because the cash register did not work, but the store could not sell fruits and vegetables anyway because the electric scales did not function. Electronic keys would not open hotel room doors; a pizza maker could not make pizzas because his electric cheese shredder did not operate; and others could not get cash because the ATMs were down.

Of course, the massive blackout was not the first time the lights had shut off. In 2000 and 2001, for example, California experienced a series of short "rolling blackouts" when it became clear that the state temporarily did not have enough power available to serve all its customers. "This is pure frustration," said Ahmed Riad when the lights went out and the toaster and espresso machine stopped working in his San Francisco coffee shop. "I just have to tell you, I felt lost,"[2] said Rosanne M. Siino, whose home office lost power for two hours and she could not use her computer. Some of the

Since the development of James Watt's steam engine (pictured) in 1769, people have increasingly relied on machines to do work.

blackouts were only fifteen minutes long, and residents were in-formed beforehand that they would occur. Even so, the disap-pearance of something that is so routinely taken for granted was hard to take. A *New York Times* reporter called it "surreal."[3]

The power shortages in both California and the Northeast were relatively brief and stemmed from problems with distribution, not supply. The blackouts spurred energy experts to rethink the best way to get electricity from power plants to clocks and air conditioners.

In the 1970s, however, concern about energy security also changed Americans' perceptions of energy in their lives. That short-age lasted for years and has influenced the lives of everyone today.

The Oil Crisis of the 1970s

In 1973 the Organization of Petroleum Exporting Countries (OPEC), led by Saudi Arabia and other Middle East countries with enormous reserves of crude oil, dramatically reduced oil exports to the United States and a few other countries. In part, the action was a response to the ongoing Arab-Israeli conflict and specifically to a war between Is-rael and Egypt in 1973. The Arab members of OPEC wanted to pun-ish the United States for its support of Israel. But the oil embargo against the United States was not as important as the overall effort to raise the price of oil by reducing the supply. OPEC's ability to raise prices was also the result of economic factors that had been building for years.

Americans had been relying more and more on imported oil, especially Middle East oil from the countries around the Persian Gulf. Drilling for this oil costs less than drilling does in most of the world, because the Middle East oil reserves are located near the earth's surface. By cutting back on their production of oil, the OPEC countries increased the price they received for oil—dramatically. Over the course of just a few months in late 1973 and early 1974, the price of oil imported into the United States jumped from $4.08 per barrel to $12.52.

For those who lived through the crisis, the most memorable re-sult, however, was not higher prices. It was the fact that gas stations did not have enough gasoline to meet consumers' demand for au-tomotive fuel. There were shortages.

People sat in their cars, waiting sometimes for hours, worried that when they did reach the pump, there would not be enough gas. In California, some gas lines were five hundred cars long. People read

Oil shortages in the 1970s led to rationing of gasoline. Here, motorists line up at a Los Angeles gas station in 1979.

books while waiting; one family whiled away the hours playing Monopoly. Performers such as mimes and musical quartets found a captive audience in the waiting cars. At other times, tensions mounted and violence resulted. One man, angered that a pregnant woman cut into the gasoline line, tried to choke her, and let the air out of her tires.

"America's insatiable appetite for energy finally came face to face with scarcity,"[4] says political scientist David Howard Davis. OPEC was not the cause of the long gas lines, however. These came about because of an American government policy that set a cap on the price of gasoline. In an effort to keep consumers from paying too much for fuel, the federal government had set limits on the prices that oil companies and gasoline retailers could charge. When costs surged because of OPEC, many oil companies and gas retailers were unable to cover the costs of supplying all the oil and gasoline that people wanted. So they cut back. This led to the shortages, which in turn caused the long gas lines. "Countries that avoided price controls, such as West Germany and Switzerland, also avoided shortages, queues, and the other perverse effects of the controls,"[5] writes Benjamin Zycher in the *Concise Encyclopedia of Economics.*

The OPEC oil embargo had enormous ripple effects on the economy of the United States. People became frightened—not just at their dependence on foreign oil but at the rising prices of all fuels, and at shortages of natural gas, which was also under price controls. The long lines fed into a much broader concern. Was the world itself running out of energy?

Running Out?

The shortages seemed to confirm the claims made in a 1972 book, *The Limits to Growth: A Report for the Club of Rome's Project on the Predicament of Mankind.* This small volume had predicted a likely disaster unless drastic changes were made. Sponsored by a group of people who were alarmed about overexploitation of the world's natural resources (called the Club of Rome), *The Limits to Growth* argued that as the world's population and its consumption of resources grew, shortages of food and non-renewable resources, including fuel, would occur, and increases in pollution would cause "irreversible damage" to the earth. The book predicted, for example, that unless trends changed, petroleum supplies could be used up by 1992. *The Limits to Growth* urged a "basic change of

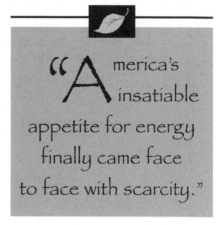

"America's insatiable appetite for energy finally came face to face with scarcity."

values and goals." People had to return to a simpler lifestyle that relied less on natural resources. If they did not, the authors argued, "the most probable result will be a rather sudden and uncontrollable decline in both population and industrial capacity."[6]

The media fueled panic with banner headlines suggesting that the United States was nearing catastrophe. It was not just fuel that

was apparently being overconsumed. As winter drew near, the cover
of the November 19, 1973, issue of *Newsweek* featured an anxious
Uncle Sam, wearing earmuffs and adorned with icicles. The head-
line read "Running Out of Everything."[7] Rising petroleum prices
led people to shift (where possible) to other fuels, and those prices,
too, went up. Furthermore, natural gas had price caps, so in addition to an increase in prices, there were shortages of natural gas as
well. And higher prices affected the many products, from televisions to plastic packaging, that have components derived from petroleum.

Although prices leveled off in the late 1970s, geopolitical factors—
the fall of the Shah of Iran in 1979 and a war between Iran and
Iraq—pushed them up again in 1979 and 1980. In 1980 a barrel
of oil cost, on average, thirty-five dollars (in today's prices, about
fifty dollars). Then, the oil crisis ended in a surprisingly simple way.
President Ronald Reagan lifted the remaining price controls on
energy in 1981. One would expect this to push prices even higher,
and for a brief time it did. Numerous commentators in newspa-
pers and magazines predicted disaster, expecting prices to sky-
rocket. But the decision proved wise. The price went up briefly,
but once oil producers could cover their costs, they began to supply more energy products. The shortages were over and supply and
demand began to come into balance.

Even with the price controls, oil prices had risen enough to encourage some oil companies to explore for more oil and natural

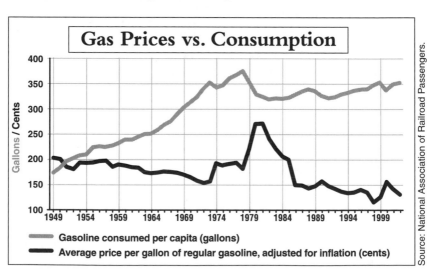

Source: National Association of Railroad Passengers.

gas. Economists S. Charles Maurice and Charles W. Smithson report that in 1981 the United States had six times the number of operating oil rigs that it had in 1971. Rising prices of energy had even led to a small boom in the mining of coal. And countries outside of OPEC had found that they could supply more oil.

Consumers responded to the shortages and high prices by conserving energy. They began to buy higher-mileage cars, reducing pressure on gasoline supplies. Some had followed President Jimmy Carter's advice to wear sweaters instead of turning the heat up in winter.

By mid-1981 prices began to fall, and in the mid-1980s the price of oil suddenly dropped—reflecting the effects of all these slight changes. Headlines that once forecast skyrocketing prices switched gears. The January 24, 1983, issue of *Newsweek* ran a piece titled "Oil Prices Hit the Skids."[8]

> When overall inflation is taken into account, the cost of oil has remained fairly steady, with occasional spikes.

In fact, prices today—in inflation-adjusted dollars—are not as high as they were in 1981. They fluctuate, and in 2003 gasoline prices moved up and down depending on short-run factors. When overall inflation is taken into account, the cost of oil has remained fairly steady, with occasional spikes. A time line over the past fifty years, adjusted for inflation, indicates that the prices of the 1970s were unusually high and that today's are generally in line with those in the 1950s.

Reflection of the Past?

The concerns about depleting natural resources that were spurred by the energy crisis of the 1970s have parallels in history. It turns out that fears of running out of energy sources recur periodically—and started even before the Industrial Revolution.

As far back as the sixteenth and seventeenth centuries, a crisis surrounded the most important source of energy in Britain—timber. Wood was necessary not just to build houses and heat homes but also to make charcoal for growing industries such as glass and metal production. These industries needed very hot fires that only charcoal (which is made by heating wood in the absence of air) could provide.

Other factors also put pressure on the forests. The British were building a navy that needed wood for its tall-masted ships. The country's population was growing rapidly, especially around London, and people needed to have houses built and heated. Because wood is bulky and hard to transport, the forests around London began to decrease. The disappearing forests "seemed to threaten Britain's existence,"[9] writes historian John U. Nef.

As the demand for wood increased and the supply fell, the price of wood rose. In fact, the higher prices rescued Britain from the crisis because they gave suppliers an incentive to find a cheaper fuel—coal.

America, too, had an early energy crisis—a shortage of whale oil. This staple from whale blubber was used to lubricate machinery and fuel lamps. But whaling expeditions reduced the number of whales, and it became more costly to find them.

The price of whale oil began to climb, which led some people to see if other substances would burn in lamps as well and, if so, to find them in quantity. In 1859 "the greatest and most lasting blow was struck at the whaling fleet,"[10] writes F.D. Ommanney: Oil was discovered in Pennsylvania. Gradually this sticky substance proved to be cheaper and more useful than whale oil.

These examples illustrate that fears of depletion can be exaggerated. Whales still roam the oceans and the United States did not run out of whale oil before something better had been found. In the cases of charcoal and whale oil, diminishing supplies led prices to rise, and those higher prices motivated suppliers and buyers to seek other fuels.

In the twentieth century, exaggerated fear of shortages occurred as well. Bjørn Lomborg, a Danish statistician, writes:

> In 1914 the US Bureau of Mines estimated that there would be oil left over for only ten years of consumption. In 1939 the Department of the Interior projected that oil would last only 13 more years, and again in 1951 it was again projected that oil would run out 13 years later. As Professor Frank Notestein of Princeton said in his later years: "We've been running out of oil ever since I've been a boy."[11]

The technology of home lighting has evolved in response to energy supplies and prices. From left are pictured: a whale-oil lamp, a rush light, candles, a grease light, a kerosene lamp, and an electric light.

Sign of the Future?

Although society has weathered previous crises, some believe that the world may not always have the energy it needs. World population has boomed. Today's population is more than 6.2 billion, and according to the World Energy Council about 1.6 billion people still live without access to any modern form of energy. If these 1.6 billion people begin to use electric power and gasoline, the risk of depletion might become very real. Some worry that there may not be another fuel to rescue modern societies if the current ones begin to gallop in price.

For example, academics Paul R. Ehrlich and Anne H. Ehrlich are worried. Since the 1960s, the Ehrlichs have been warning about the dangers of excess population growth and overconsumption of natural resources, including fuel. In their 1991 book *Healing the Planet* they write that "humanity now faces both unprecedented catastrophe and a last opportunity to bequeath to all our descendants a decent planet to live on." [12] As part of their prescription, they argue that "the rich countries must wean themselves from their addiction to fossil fuels." [13]

Unlike trees and plants, oil and natural gas are resources that are not renewable— they do not grow back.

Indeed, the world continues to consume greater and greater quantities of oil with each passing year. Unlike trees and plants, oil and natural gas are resources that are not renewable—they do not grow back. Still, the world seems to have an abundant supply of fossil fuels. Whether society uses them depends on price and current technology.

Scientists measure the amount of fuel that is available by proven reserves. Currently, scientists estimate that the world has proven reserves of crude oil that will last about forty-five years. But proven reserves are not the same as petroleum in the ground. Proven reserves are the amount of a resource that is known to be recoverable under current conditions. Those conditions include the current price. When the price changes, the size of the proven reserves changes.

For example, if gasoline were to drop to ten cents a gallon, proven reserves would plummet. Oil producers would stop pumping oil because they would not earn enough to cover their costs. In a parallel way, if gasoline became more expensive, proven reserves would increase. At the higher price, oil that would have been too expensive to pump (and therefore not previously counted as proven reserves) could instead be sold profitably. Robert L. Bradley Jr., an energy analyst who heads the Institute for Energy Research, points out that today's proven oil reserves are fifteen times greater than they were estimated to be in 1948—even though we have consumed eleven times the 1948 estimated proven reserves. Higher prices and new technology have led to larger proven reserves.

Whenever fears about dependence on foreign sources arise, Americans can look to their own country and to the world's most abundant fuel—coal. Although coal cannot directly replace petroleum as a source of gasoline, it can be used for some energy needs. Coal accounts for roughly 50 percent of all electricity production in the United States, and with vast quantities of coal untapped, it could provide much more.

According to the Energy Information Administration, the world has about 1,089 billion tons in proven coal reserves, which can last another two centuries. Probable reserves—the reserves that would be tapped if prices were higher—are much larger. Robert L. Bradley Jr. thinks that they could last nearly two millennia (1,884 years) at current consumption rates.

There is, of course, an important problem with coal. It is dirty. Although new technologies enable electric utilities to reduce their emissions from burning coal, the fuel still produces contaminants,

Surface coal mining is safer for coal workers than deep mining, but the resulting deep, open pits such as this one in Manzhouli, China, can scar the earth.

and its dusty nature makes it difficult to handle. Coal is also dangerous to those who mine it. Although the industry is far safer than it used to be, twenty-seven coal workers died in 2002, and an increase in the use of coal would probably raise that number. Surface mining is safer than deep mining, but it has environmental impacts. Giant machinery creates deep open pits from which the coal is removed. This kind of mining scars the earth, and repairing the site after the mine is closed can be extremely expensive. Yet the fact that it remains ample in supply under the ground throughout the world means that the world will still have a reliable source of energy for centuries to come.

Conclusion

Are Americans running out of energy? Yes and no. Some people still worry about long-term depletion of energy, but for most Americans, the greatest concern is that they are too dependent on foreign sources of fuel, especially petroleum. Running out of energy is an issue related more to social and political problems than to resource availability. In either case, concern about running out raises the question of whether Americans can find new sources of energy. That is a big question.

CHAPTER 2

Should Public Lands Be Opened to Energy Development?

T he windswept Arctic National Wildlife Refuge (ANWR) in the northeastern corner of Alaska has been a subject of controversy for nearly two decades. Home to caribou, polar bears, and other wild animals, this nearly 20-million-acre refuge in the Arctic tundra is also believed to hold billions of barrels of oil.

The federal government owns ANWR. Most of the territory has been designated as off-limits to oil drilling. But there is a continuing conflict over whether the government should allow oil drilling on a small northern portion of the refuge—about 8 percent of the total acreage—called the coastal plain.

Congress created the wildlife refuge in 1980 as part of the Alaska National Lands Act. It is one of more than five hundred wildlife refuges around the country. They all have as their chief goal the protection of wildlife, but they are not necessarily meant to be pristine habitats. For example, hunting is allowed on many refuges, and some oil and gas exploration or production is allowed at thirty-six refuges, according to the U.S. General Accounting Office (some of these are ocean areas off the U.S. coast).

When Congress created ANWR, it divided the refuge into three parts. Eight million acres are wilderness, a designation that forbids any commercial development, and 10 million acres are protected as a wildlife refuge; although this part of the refuge is not as tightly restricted as wilderness is, oil exploration and production are not allowed. Congress could not quite decide what to do with the remaining 1.5 million coastal acres known as Section 1002. Not quite ready to open it up for oil production, Congress did not want to close it off completely, either. So the members reached a compromise. They decided that the coastal plain can be opened for exploration and drilling only if Congress votes approval.

Periodically, efforts have been made to open ANWR, but the debate is fierce. Most of the discussion centers on the possible environmental harm caused by drilling.

This political battle over ANWR illustrates the larger controversy over *all* sources of energy such as coal, natural gas, and nuclear power. Yes, consumers may want to have more secure supplies of energy, but during the processes of fuel extraction, consumption, and use, the environment is changed, sometimes permanently. Environmental effects may be so severe, some argue, that these energy sources should be used only sparingly. People are divided on the issue.

The Arctic Refuge Debate

During the 1980s Congress almost allowed drilling on the coastal plain of ANWR. Petroleum was already produced in Alaska's North Slope and transported via a pipeline through Alaska to Valdez. Building that pipeline had been hotly contested in its day, but since the pipeline began carrying oil in 1978, worries had subsided. The impact of the trans-Alaska pipeline on the tundra and its wildlife seemed small. Caribou, the animals of greatest concern because they migrated along the pipeline, seemed to be thriving. Their numbers grew, and sometimes they were photographed around the pipeline. When the herd migrates in the summer, the animals sometimes walk beneath or near the pipelines, which are five feet above ground. (Scientists believe that the pipelines provide shade and relief for the caribou from the annoying flies that come out in late June or early July.) And to some extent, people had shifted their attention to issues other than the environment.

But in 1989 attitudes changed. The *Exxon Valdez,* an oil tanker carrying petroleum piped from the North Slope, ran aground off Alaska's coast, spilling nearly 11 million gallons of oil into the biologically rich waters of Prince William Sound. It was the worst oil spill in the history of the United States.

A wildlife rescue worker handles a guillemot covered in oil from the 1989 Exxon Valdez *spill.*

Oil oozed onto the surrounding beaches, eventually touching thirteen hundred miles of shoreline, threatening land animals and sea life. Fish, sea otters, and migratory birds died, many of them caked in oil. Although a massive cleanup followed, the *Exxon Valdez* brought the environmental hazards of oil drilling to the forefront of American awareness.

Although spills kill birds and fish and can damage miles of beaches, recovery generally occurs over time. Shortly after the *Exxon Valdez* spill, the Congressional Research Service, an arm of Congress, reported on its study of six major oil spills of the previous two decades. The agency concluded that the long-term impact of the spills was "relatively modest and, as far as can be determined, of relatively short duration." [14] That may be reassuring to some, but it does not mean that oil spills are not a problem. Since 1960 more than 950 spills, with more than 10,000 gallons of oil each, have poured into the ocean.

Ever since the *Exxon Valdez*, Americans have been wary of pumping more oil from Alaska. Oil spills can occur through pipeline breaks or leaks, as well as from oil tankers, and such ruptures could harm Alaskan wildlife. In a 2001 letter to President George W. Bush, more than five hundred scientists and resource managers petitioned to keep ANWR free from oil drilling. They argued that the coastal plain "forms a vital component of the biological diversity of the refuge"[15] and that it should be managed in the same way as the rest of the refuge— that is, without drilling.

> Since 1960 more than 950 spills, with more than 10,000 gallons of oil each, have poured into the ocean.

The chief environmental issue is whether the disruption caused by exploration (including seismic exploration) and drilling will harm the animals that live on the tundra. The area is rich in grizzly bears, polar bears, caribou, wolverines, other mammals, and many migratory birds. Alaska represents one of the last remote and relatively untouched parts of the United States. A study by the Clinton administration (which opposed drilling) said that the "irreplaceable and enduring value of the Arctic Refuge to the nation as a world-class natural area and wilderness is far greater than the short-term economic gain to be garnered from industrial development."[16] Wildlife organizations such as the Sierra Club and the Defenders of Wildlife cast doubt on the willingness of oil producers to protect wildlife. "You can't trust big oil," says a video sponsored by Defenders of Wildlife and available on its website. "Drilling would upset the Arctic's fragile web of life. . . . Oil and wildlife don't mix."[17]

Supporters counter by saying that Alaska is enormous—the largest of the fifty states—and millions of acres of land have already been set aside to protect wildlife. Alaska alone has sixteen national wildlife refuges, and drilling on Section 1002 would take up just a small part of one of them.

Perhaps the longest-running debate surrounds caribou, the large antlered animals that migrate long distances across Alaska. The coastal plain of ANWR includes the major calving grounds for the Porcupine herd of 130,000 caribou. Some biologists fear that their calving will be disrupted by oil development. They point to some studies showing that the Central Arctic herd, a smaller group of caribou that calve in and around the oil field at Prudhoe Bay, may have been affected by the drilling there. These studies indicate that some caribou, especially females, stay away from the oil structures. If the Porcupine herd did the same, they might have problems finding a place to have their offspring.

The coastal plain of ANWR includes a caribou calving ground. Some biologists fear that oil development will negatively affect the herd.

However, these studies do not show any reduction in the size of the Central Arctic herd, which fluctuates naturally due to changes in conditions such as weather, parasites, and hunting. In 1972 the Alaska Fish and Game Department estimated that the herd numbered three thousand caribou. In 1992 it was between twenty-five and twenty-seven thousand and has not changed much since. Critics respond to this optimistic view, however, by saying that the Porcupine herd is four times as large and the protected plain they use as a calving ground is smaller than the land used by the Central Arctic herd.

In addition to emphasizing the apparently thriving health of the Central Arctic herd, proponents also point out that the amount of surface land directly affected by oil exploration and development would be small, possibly only two thousand acres, compared with the total of 1.5 million acres in the coastal plain. Some geologists believe most of the oil in Section 1002 probably can be reached by drilling in one central location rather than having oil rigs scattered throughout the coastal plain. Thus very little land would be disturbed by oil rigs and other production equipment. Whether this conventional wisdom about ANWR is actually true, however, depends on what is found if actual exploration occurs.

Another argument in favor of drilling is that much of the construction would take place in the winter. Trucks would move cargo on ice roads so that they would not actually touch the grassy tundra, which many consider fragile. These roads would melt in the summer.

Second only to the worries about the caribou are those surrounding polar bears. These bears make their dens either on sea ice or in the snowbanks on land. Their cubs are born in midwinter and cannot survive outside the dens until early spring. Disruption such as seismic exploration, which uses small explosions and vibrations to help scientists study the structure and composition of the earth under the soil surface, could cause the females to flee from their dens when their cubs are too small to survive the rigors of the outside environment. "Polar bears have a low productive rate and any activity that reduces denning success could cause a population decline," says Jack Lentfer, a retired biologist who directed polar bear research for the Alaska Department of

Fish and Game and the U.S. Fish and Wildlife Service between 1967 and 1977. In his view, "oil production from the Arctic National Wildlife Refuge does not justify the risk that development poses to polar bears and other wildlife." [18]

But equally credible scientists suggest that most of the likely impacts on denning bears could be dealt with. Steven Amstrup, who has been the Polar Bear Project leader for the U.S. Geological Survey (USGS) since 1980, says that while exploration and development pose a genuine threat to polar bears, available data suggest most of the threats can be addressed with careful management of human activities. "Our studies have identified the kinds of habitats in which polar bears prefer to den, and we also have learned when they enter and leave their dens," he says. "Therefore, in the case of denning polar bears, we have the ability to

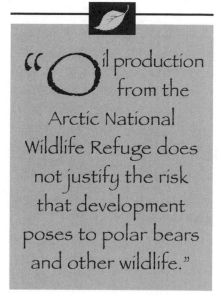

"Oil production from the Arctic National Wildlife Refuge does not justify the risk that development poses to polar bears and other wildlife."

manage oilfield-related activities both temporally and spatially to minimize impacts." [19] For example, companies doing exploration can be required to avoid denning areas until early April when polar bears leave their dens and go back out to hunt on the sea ice.

The fight over ANWR has become quite bitter, with disputants even arguing over whether the coastal plain is much of an environmental treasure. "There are no majestic mountains, beautiful forests, or other natural wonders in the coastal plain area of the Arctic Refuge, where the actual oil prospects lie," writes Robert H. Nelson, a professor of economics who studies natural resource issues. "This area is a barren and desolate stretch of tundra bordering the Arctic Ocean and dark much of the time." [20]

Others agree that the flat tundra of the coastal plain is unlike the dramatic mountains typical of many of America's national parks, but argue that it is no less worth preserving in its natural state. William H. Meadows, president of the Wilderness Society, says that "its value lies in its very wildness, and wildness in turn is valuable

Many nature enthusiasts argue that the barren tundra of the Arctic National Wildlife Refuge is as worthy of preservation as America's other national parks.

precisely because it is difficult to understand, impossible to capture." Visiting the coastal plain, he found "wonders everywhere I looked— vast flocks of birds, brants, plovers, birds I had never seen. We came eye to eye with an Arctic fox. . . . We saw the sedges, wildflowers, and dwarf trees that had succeeded in their struggle to survive." [21] Ornithologist David Sibley calls the refuge "a whole and natural place, a true wilderness, where the birds are at home and we are visitors." [22]

The USGS estimates that ANWR has between 4.3 and 11.8 billion barrels of recoverable oil, with an average estimate of 7.7 billion barrels. To put that into perspective, the United States uses about 7 billion barrels of oil a year, so the total amount of oil may be about equal to one year's use of oil in the United States. Another way to look at it is that the Prudhoe Bay development, which is considered a rich source of oil, has pumped out nearly 13 billion barrels in the quarter of a century it has been in operation. Those who oppose drilling tend to minimize the quantity in the coastal plain; those who favor drilling tend to emphasize the output over the next decade or two if drilling is allowed.

Alaskan Eskimos are divided over drilling. The northern Inupiat Eskimos, some of whom live near Prudhoe Bay, where oil production has gone on since the 1970s, generally support opening up the coastal plain to drilling. The revenues from oil development have modernized their homes and supported their educational system. "ANWR holds resources that can be extracted safely with care and concern for the entire eco-system it encompasses,"[23] says Benjamin P. Nageak, an Alaskan Inupiat.

In contrast, the Gwich'n, who are poorer, live at the southern edge of the refuge, and have not had much contact with Alaskan oil activities, oppose development. They are caribou hunters who rely on the Porcupine herd of caribou. They are understandably concerned that the drilling might lead to population declines in the migrating caribou on which their livelihood depends. "We aren't antidevelopment. We aren't environmentalists," Gideon James, a former Gwich'n chief, told the *Wall Street Journal.* "We just don't want any drilling where the caribou have their calves."[24]

On March 19, 2003, Congress agreed with the Gwich'n and other opponents of drilling. It voted to continue the ban on oil drilling in ANWR.

Other Sites

Disagreement over allowing oil drilling in the ANWR is only one of many conflicts over how much public land will be used for energy exploration and development. The U.S. government owns nearly a third of the land mass of the United States. Much of that land is in the West,

The U.S. government owns nearly a third of the land mass of the United States.

where rich deposits of coal, natural gas, and oil are found. According to David Morehouse, senior petroleum geologist with the Energy Information Administration, federal lands—including offshore federal lands under the oceans—hold 60 percent of the nation's reserves of crude oil and 52 percent of the nation's natural gas reserves. Federal regulations determine how much of this energy may be produced.

Federal and state governments share control over the continental shelf, the resource-rich ground underneath the nation's coastal waters. These areas are largely off-limits to development, partly because of opposition from residents of Florida, Washington, Oregon, and California, who worry that they will have to see oil rigs in the distance.

> Over time, the federal government has been closing off more and more of its natural resources to development.

Over time, the federal government has been closing off more and more of its natural resources to development. The 1964 Wilderness Act, for example, set aside 9 million acres as wilderness—land that from then on would be preserved with minimal human impacts. By the year 2000, U.S. wilderness had expanded to 105 million acres. When all federal parks, refuges, and other protected lands are added up, 450 million acres of land—an area twice the size of Texas—are strictly limited in use, according to public lands researcher Holly Lippke Fretwell. These set-asides reduce the potential for energy production on federal land.

The U.S. government also purchases land and accepts donations, mostly for parks and refuges and other lands where energy production is not allowed. According to Fretwell the major agencies that manage federal land have increased their holdings by 33.6 million acres since 1960. This is an area almost the size of Florida. Many people approve of this expansion of protected lands. Carl Pope, executive director of the Sierra Club, said in 1999, "A major increase in federal funding for land acquisition has long been needed." [25] But such acquisition also means less land for oil and gas and coal production.

The Bush administration has taken steps to expand exploration and drilling, instructing land managers to see whether unnecessary restrictions are holding back development of the reserves in the West. But some environmental groups are wary. Pete Morton, a resource economist with the Wilderness Society, told the Associated Press: "It's not that we're opposed to drilling in a responsible manner. But the BLM [Bureau of Land Management, one of the agencies that are reviewing their regulations] has not adequately explained why we need to expedite these processes." [26]

One reason for the greater interest in exploring for natural gas in the United States is the fact that it is an environmentally attractive alternative to coal. The majority of power plants currently in the planning stages are expected to use natural gas rather than coal. The reason is simple: Natural gas burns the most cleanly; it emits minimal pollution (only nitrogen oxides) when it burns, and it produces less carbon dioxide than other fossil fuels.

This growth in demand has pushed up the price of natural gas. If new sources of natural gas cannot be found, prices may remain high for years to come. The uncertainty of future supplies spurred the influential chairman of the Federal Reserve Bank, Alan Greenspan, to recommend more importation of liquefied natural gas from other countries. Liquefied natural gas is natural gas that

Federal Reserve chairman Alan Greenspan testifies before the Senate Energy and Natural Resources Committee about the increase in natural gas prices.

has been condensed so that it takes up less space than in its gaseous state, and thus can be carried by tankers. Greenspan noted that greater imports would "expose us to possibly insecure sources of freight supply, as it has for oil,"[27] although he added that natural gas reserves are not as concentrated in the Middle East as oil reserves are.

Always Destructive?

Although finding fossil fuels always requires some environmental disruption, the techniques for obtaining oil and natural gas have become increasingly sophisticated. Companies can minimize the effects on the surrounding surfaces and, after digging has been completed, return the land to pretty much the way it was. For example, Avery Island off Louisiana's gulf coast is rich in oil. In the 1980s the owners of this island wanted to exploit it but also preserve its unique qualities. This is the island where the peppers that go into McIlhenny's Tabasco sauce are grown; the island is also a tourist attraction and has a wildlife preserve.

The company that was to retrieve the oil chose to build a single well pad in the center of the pepper fields. From that pad it drilled vertically for one mile; then drilling turned horizontally for as far as two miles in order to tap into the oil reserves. "When the drilling was completed two years later, all parties were happy with the results," says Reid Lea, an engineer who worked on the project. "Several highly productive wells had been completed and little or no residual environmental impact was created."[28]

Evidence that energy development can be relatively benign also comes from the National Audubon Society. For many years this environmental organization obtained natural gas from wells located in its Paul J. Rainey Sanctuary, a twenty-six-thousand-acre preserve the Audubon Society owns, also in southern Louisiana. The sanctuary is a preserve for more than one hundred thousand migrating snow geese as well as ducks, wading birds, deer, and fish. Although natural gas drilling occurred for nearly forty-five years, no significant harm to wildlife was ever detected. That was partly because Audubon required the drilling companies to take special precautions, such as staying out during nesting season. "We know of no other instance where oil or gas drilling operations in a protected area are subject to such stringent standards as those in place at Rainey,"[29] wrote the president of Audubon, John Flicker, in 1995.

Completed in 1977, the trans-Alaska pipeline carries oil eight hundred miles across Alaska to the port at Valdez.

The organization was able to earn more than $25 million in royalties from the sale of the natural gas. Audubon stopped drilling in 1999, when the natural gas reserves became no longer economically productive.

Audubon's success with its natural gas on Rainey does not lead it to favor oil drilling in Alaska, however. Audubon president Flicker wrote that "the massive scale of the oil drilling, exploration, and industry development being proposed in the Arctic National Wildlife Refuge would destroy the unique wilderness quality of the 1.5 million acre coastal plain forever." [30] Another Audubon official distinguishes between drilling in the warm, humid climate of Louisiana, where vegetation grows easily, and drilling in the cold tundra of Alaska, where grasses might have difficulty revegetating. Whether Audubon's views on drilling would change if it owned ANWR and could ensure the refuge's environmental integrity is an unanswered question.

Conclusion

Tempers flare over more drilling in the United States, especially in Alaska but also in the Rocky Mountains. Given the strong feelings and the political nature of decision making, it seems unlikely that retrieving more oil and natural gas will be a major route to U.S. energy independence. How severe a problem that poses remains to be seen.

CHAPTER 3

How Harmful Are Current Energy Sources?

Searching for and digging out oil, coal, or natural gas are not the only ways that fossil fuels harm the environment. The combustion of these fuels has impacts as well, largely through air pollution.

Today's air pollution comes primarily from two sources: automobiles in cities and the combustion of coal in electric power plants. The smog caused by automobiles is the most notorious pollution because it spreads through cities as a brown haze, visible to everyone. In contrast, many power plants are located some distance away from urban centers so that most people see them only rarely. Both sources, however, contribute pollutants.

Smog is found in large cities such as Los Angeles, Denver, and Houston. It has its origins in automobile exhaust, which produces particles and volatile gases that react with one another in sunlight (often called photochemical smog), forming haze. Ozone is one of the major byproducts of these chemical reactions and a major component of smog.

To reduce smog Congress has required automakers to lessen vehicle pollutant emissions, and as a result today's cars emit about 90 percent less pollution than cars did in the 1970s (although trucks lag behind). In addition, the Environmental Protection Agency (EPA) has required new formulations of gasoline that emit fewer pollutants. Cities that have high levels of ozone and other

Automobile emissions and sunlight react to form ozone, a major component of the smog that plagues some U.S. cities such as Los Angeles (pictured).

air pollution have also taken a variety of steps, from automobile inspection programs to efforts to spur carpooling.

But that is not enough to eliminate smog, especially in cities where weather and geographical factors keep natural breezes from cleaning the air. Houston and parts of Southern California are the most serious violators of the EPA's standards for smog.

How serious air pollution is in these cities remains a subject of debate. For example, the American Lung Association says that 49 percent of all Americans live in areas with unhealthy levels of ozone. But Joel Schwartz of the Reason Public Policy Institute disputes this calculation. His research shows that the level of noncompliance with EPA standards is much lower. For example, the Lung Association says that Los Angeles County exceeded the EPA's standard for ozone an average of thirty-five days per year between 1999 and 2001. But Schwartz points out that Los Angeles County has fourteen different monitoring stations. The Lung Association treats a violation at each station as if it affects the entire county. Typically, however, only part—and sometimes a small part—of the population is affected by such a violation.

The second major source of air pollution in the United States is emissions from electricity-producing power plants. About half of these plants are fueled by coal, and coal combustion produces numerous chemicals, such as sulfur dioxide and nitrogen oxides, as well as particles of unburned coal. These substances can harm human health, vegetation, and buildings near their sources. In addition, these particles can cause acid rain.

Acid rain used to be a frightening thing, partly because the name evokes the image of battery acid falling from the sky. Acid rain is not nearly as extreme as that, however. In fact, all rainwater is slightly acidic because of the carbon dioxide naturally in the air. That is, it has a higher than normal number of hydrogen ions. Acid rain refers to rain that has been made more acidic by human-caused pollutants.

The federal government conducted a ten-year study of acid rain, completed in 1990, and concluded that its impact is relatively small. The study, entitled the National Acid Precipitation Assessment Program or NAPAP, concluded that acid rain may have damaged some red spruce trees in the Appalachian Mountains, but these trees were also under stress from wind and cold temperatures. It probably contributed to the acidity of some small lakes in New York, making them unable to support fish, but it does not have the widespread impacts that many people thought it did.

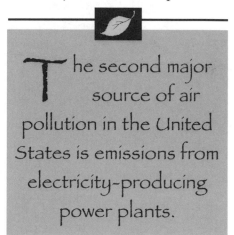

The second major source of air pollution in the United States is emissions from electricity-producing power plants.

The EPA's greatest concern with air pollution now appears to be with very small particles known as fine particulates. These tiny airborne particles can enter the lungs and cause respiratory problems. A series of studies by the Harvard School of Public Health concluded that when the number of these particulates increased in certain big cities, the number of deaths increased as well. These findings are still controversial, even a dozen years after they appeared, but they led the EPA to issue tougher regulations on power plants in 1997. The regulations, which go into effect in 2004, require power plants to reduce emissions of pollutants even further.

Although air pollution remains a problem in the United States, it has declined drastically. A study by the Pacific Research Institute, based on EPA statistics, shows that the amount of major pol-

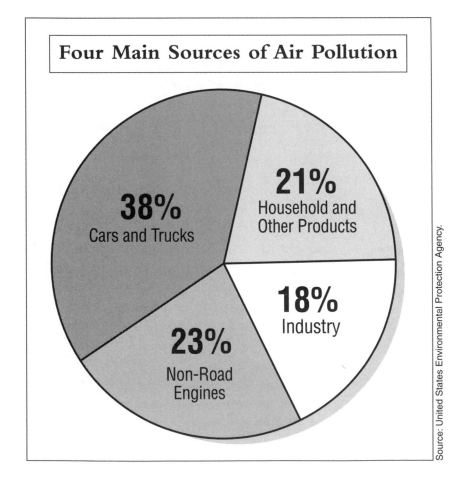

Four Main Sources of Air Pollution

38% Cars and Trucks

21% Household and Other Products

18% Industry

23% Non-Road Engines

Source: United States Environmental Protection Agency.

lutants such as sulfur dioxide, carbon monoxide, and lead are much lower today than they were in the mid-1970s, even though the nation's population—and subsequently driving—has increased dramatically since then. For example, ozone has declined by 33 percent, sulfur dioxide by 67 percent, and lead by 97 percent. (Ozone levels, however, have remained about the same for the past decade.)

Air pollution has been declining ever since the 1920s, largely through a combination of private choices, new technologies, and local regulations. Until the 1920s many people in the United States burned coal in their homes, which kept cities sooty and smoky. But then coal was replaced with cleaner-burning fuels such as fuel oil and natural gas. Indur Goklany, author of *Clearing the Air*, a his-

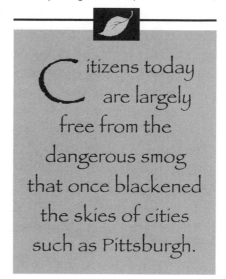

Citizens today are largely free from the dangerous smog that once blackened the skies of cities such as Pittsburgh.

torical study of air pollution in the United States, points out that only 14 million people used natural gas in their homes in 1932; by 1951, the number had more than tripled, reaching 51 million.

Industry, too, sought new fuels and new technologies. Engineers found ways to burn coal more cleanly, causing less smoke, and companies switched to less polluting fuels. Progress will continue, partly because of regulations already on the books and because companies do not want to be known as polluters. Citizens today are largely free from the dangerous smog that once blackened the skies of cities such as Pittsburgh.

Global Warming

Skies are brighter, but another anxiety about fossil fuel combustion has gripped Americans. Global warming, writes energy specialist Jack M. Hollander, "has thrown a huge roadblock in the path of continuing growth in use of fossil fuels by both developing and developed countries."[31] To understand its importance, it is necessary to understand the connection between fossil fuels and warmer temperatures.

During the past one hundred years, the average global temperatures on the earth's surface have gone up about 0.6 degrees Celsius, or about 1 degree Fahrenheit. This has not been a continual increase: For example, temperatures fell between 1938 and the mid-1970s, but then moved upward again. Scientists are worried that burning fossil fuels is contributing to this increase.

Fossil fuels include large quantities of carbon. When the fuels are burned, carbon and oxygen combine to create carbon dioxide, which is released into the atmosphere. Carbon dioxide is not a pollutant; that is, it does not cause any direct harm on its own, and in fact, plants need it to grow.

But more carbon dioxide in the atmosphere intensifies the greenhouse effect. This is the tendency of water vapor and gases such as carbon dioxide to trap heat from the surface of the earth. This greenhouse effect is natural; without it, the earth would be cold and almost uninhabitable. But the more fossil fuels that are burned, the more carbon dioxide is added to the atmosphere, and the more powerful the greenhouse effect.

What scientists do not know is whether the effect of carbon dioxide is small or large. They are constantly studying what fac-

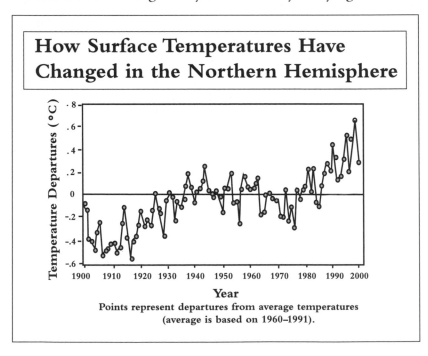

How Surface Temperatures Have Changed in the Northern Hemisphere

Points represent departures from average temperatures (average is based on 1960–1991).

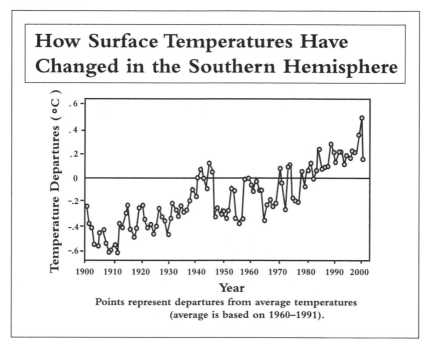

How Surface Temperatures Have Changed in the Southern Hemisphere

Year

Points represent departures from average temperatures
(average is based on 1960–1991).

tors affect climate change, and their studies abound with uncertainty. Most predictions about future warming are made by computer models of the global climate that are known to have serious weaknesses in describing the ways that climate operates.

One uncertainty stems from the pattern of cooling temperatures between 1938 and the mid-1970s. This decline in average temperatures is puzzling because the major increases in atmospheric carbon dioxide occurred after 1938, not before. If the carbon dioxide was causing the warming, why did it get cooler? And there is the puzzling fact that temperatures a few miles above the earth, measured by satellites and weather balloons, have hardly budged since 1980.

As scientists understand climate, carbon dioxide itself has just a small greenhouse effect. For temperatures to rise dramatically, the slightly warmer temperature has to increase water vapor in the air, and the water vapor, not the carbon dioxide, raises temperatures more. But one prominent scientist, Richard Lindzen of the Massachusetts Institute of Technology, contends that if the tropics warmed, they would change air circulation patterns, bringing drier air from the upper atmosphere levels. With drier air and less water vapor, the earth might cool instead of warm.

Another factor that could change the computer forecasts is air pollution, which is declining in North America but increasing elsewhere. Pollutants can lower temperatures because small dark particles reflect the Sun's rays back into space, cooling the earth. And even the Sun itself changes the intensity of its heat in long cycles. Some scientists think that the natural changes in the Sun's heat may explain changes in climate better than the addition of carbon dioxide.

> # Many researchers have accepted the claim that global warming is imminent and dangerous.

These uncertainties are widely recognized, and there are many more. Even so, many researchers have accepted the claim that global warming is imminent and dangerous. "Evidence is growing that this trend will lead to changes in atmospheric circulation that correlate with increased occurrence of extreme weather events, such as storms, droughts, floods, and heat waves,"[32] wrote the editors of *Nature,* an influential scientific journal, in August 2003. To them, the possibilities are serious enough to cut back on fossil fuels.

Backed by environmental activists and supported by the media, the push for reducing fossil fuel use has affected politicians around the world. The major political action so far has been for governments of many nations to sign an agreement known as the Kyoto Protocol (it was formulated at a meeting in Kyoto, Japan, in 1997). The protocol spells out steps that the industrialized countries will take to reduce their emissions of carbon dioxide (if enough countries sign it so that it goes into effect). For example, the United States would have to reduce its emissions of carbon dioxide by 7 percent below the amount it was producing in 1990 (which means quite a cutback, because emissions have gone up since 1990).

If the Kyoto Protocol becomes law, companies would try to use less fuel, and would also seek out fuels that produce less carbon dioxide. Natural gas (which emits less carbon dioxide than other fossil fuels) would become the preferred fossil fuel, at least initially, and the search for noncarbon-based fuels could open markets to alternatives such as solar and wind power. Fuel costs for everyone would go up, probably causing slower growth in the economy as a whole, and some companies are likely to go out of business because of the higher fuel costs.

The protocol is not yet in effect. President George W. Bush decided not to support the protocol, even though his predecessor, Bill Clinton, had signed it. In spite of this decision, Bush is allowing the EPA to develop programs that will reward companies that voluntarily cut back on their use of fossil fuels. Numerous state governments have become involved, too, trying to persuade companies to reduce their use of fossil fuels in the name of global warming.

Ironically, however, even meeting the Kyoto goals—which would be especially difficult for the United States because of its high energy use—will not have an appreciable effect on global warming. James E. Hansen, a prestigious government scientist, has written with others, "Thirty Kyotos may be needed to reduce warming to an acceptable level."[33] According to one estimate, the reduction in average temperatures by 2040 would be 0.06 degrees Celsius.

Although the views of scientists and environmental organizations affect policy decisions, public concern is probably the biggest driver of political action on global warming. That concern escalated when the 1990s and the early twenty-first century experienced a series of hot years, some of them the hottest years since formal records of global temperatures began during the second half of the 1800s. But if the torrid summers end, public opinion could back off from its absorption with global warming. Whether this is good or bad for the long term is another matter, but public indifference could ease pressure to reduce fossil fuel use.

Nuclear Power—Safe or Risky?

One widely used source of energy does not produce either smog or carbon dioxide. It provides approximately 20 percent of the electricity used in the United States and could provide much more. Yet, rightly or wrongly, nuclear power is the most feared energy source of all.

Nuclear power produces energy by splitting uranium atoms. It has its origins in the government program that created the atomic bomb in World War II. After the war, the newfound knowledge about the atom led to the use of "atoms for peace" through nuclear energy.

Many Americans fear a catastrophe that could spew dangerous radiation, and the potential for such a catastrophe does exist. In 1979, an accident occurred at a nuclear power plant, Three Mile Island, near Harrisburg, Pennsylvania. A plume of radioactive steam was emitted, stirring enormous fears that have not yet abated.

The accident started with a problem with the cooling system early in the morning of March 28, 1979. This system is designed to keep the reactor core—the place where uranium atoms are split and heat is produced—from getting too hot. When a backup

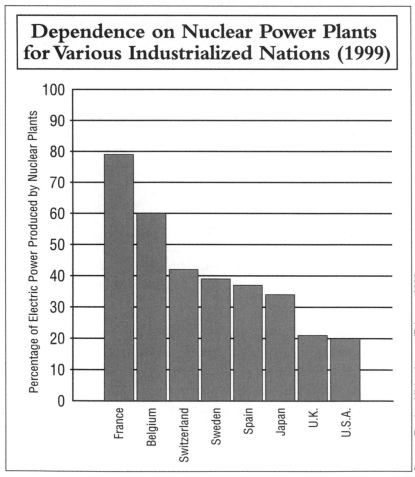

Dependence on Nuclear Power Plants for Various Industrialized Nations (1999)

Source: *Foreign Affairs*, January/February 2000.

system failed, the reactor automatically shut down, as it was designed to do. Because the pressure of the reactor core was high, a valve opened automatically, releasing hot water into a drainage tank.

But the valve failed to close, and the operators of the plant did not know it. This flaw—mundane when compared with sophisticated issues about how nuclear plants are designed—was the key link in the chain of events. With the valve stuck, so much water flowed into the drainage tank that one of its components broke, spilling thousands of gallons of radioactive water into the containment building that surrounds the reactor. With the core lacking enough water to cover it completely, it overheated and some fuel rods burst, adding radioactive contamination to the water. Some contaminated water was pumped to tanks in an adjacent building, from which radioactive gases escaped into the environment.

The immediate crisis was resolved by the end of the day, when employees figured out what happened and covered the reactor core with coolant water. Many people, however, including government officials, still feared the possibility of a hydrogen explosion. That evening, Walter Cronkite, then the anchor on the *CBS Evening News,* called it "the first step in a nuclear nightmare." [34]

Lack of information fueled panic. Residents near Three Mile Island left their homes. "Schools closed, families packed up and gasoline stations did a brisk business as an estimated 50,000 to 60,000 people headed away, for the weekend at least," [35] wrote *Newsweek.* On March 30, the governor of Pennsylvania recommended that pregnant women and preschool children who lived within five miles of the unit evacuate the area, and many did.

No injuries or deaths occurred from Three Mile Island. President Jimmy Carter quickly appointed a commission (headed by John Kemeny, president of Dartmouth College) to study the accident. The Kemeny commission concluded that the plume of radioactive gases had exposed those who lived within five miles of Three Mile Island to an additional 10 percent of the amount of radiation they would normally receive in a year. (For people within fifty miles, the figure was just 1 percent.) The commission also stated that there was never any chance of a major explosion. Subsequent

On the second anniversary of the Three Mile Island accident, demonstrators in Harrisburg, Pennsylvania, protest the use of nuclear power.

studies have been unable to identify any long-term effects of the Three Mile Island accident. The Columbia University Division of Epidemiology reported in 1990, eleven years later, that it could detect no increases in cancer as a result of the accident. Nevertheless, the accident stirred up intense fear of nuclear power.

And then in April 1986 a terrible nuclear accident did occur. The place was Chernobyl, a nuclear power plant located in the Ukraine, then part of the Soviet Union. Technicians had shut down the plant's safety systems in order to conduct an experiment. These actions and others led to a chain reaction in the nuclear core, causing a series of explosions that spewed radioactive material into the atmosphere over a period of ten days.

The magnitude of this disaster was enormous. Thirty-two people died as a direct result of the accident, and 140 people suffered radiation sickness or other effects, leading to more deaths. The amount of radiation emitted into the atmosphere was several times greater than the radiation from the atomic bombs dropped during World War II on the Japanese cities of Hiroshima and Nagasaki. Another way to describe the impact is in curies, a measure of radioactivity. The explosions released almost 100 million curies of radioactivity; Three Mile Island had released 15 curies.

The effects of the disaster are still being felt. The Nuclear Energy Agency, a European organization that has studied Chernobyl, reports that there has been a significant increase in thyroid cancer among those who were children in the region when the accident occurred, and possibly among adults. Other cancers have not increased, however.

Experts differentiate Chernobyl from other nuclear power plants, and some doubt that the accident is directly relevant to nuclear safety in the rest of the world. The Soviet Union operated under a central government that had little concern for its citizens, and the Chernobyl design has never been used outside Russia, Lithuania, and the Ukraine. It was originally adopted for nuclear plants in Siberia, far from any major city. In fact, when

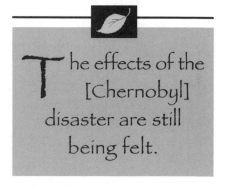

The effects of the [Chernobyl] disaster are still being felt.

construction was about to start in the Ukraine, only sixty miles from Kiev, some people did raise questions about the design.

As far back as 1972, Gregori Medvedev, an engineer at the Chernobyl plant (who later wrote a book about Chernobyl), questioned the safety of the reactor design and knew of one scholar who had voiced objections to the Ukrainian minister of energy. But such doubts were ignored. "That accident was the product of an atrocious Soviet reactor and plant design [RBMK-1000] that would never have been approved for commercial use in any Western country," [36] says energy analyst Jack M. Hollander.

Two scholars who have studied nuclear power, Joseph G. Morone and Edward J. Woodhouse, have identified several design flaws in the plant that caused the accident to be far more severe than Three Mile Island. For one thing, the workers in the Soviet plant were able to override the safety system. Then, when they tried to stop the reaction in the core, the system only gave them four seconds—not enough time to insert control rods that would slow

The effects of the Chernobyl accident are still being felt today. Here, French scientists analyze levels of radioactivity near the power plant.

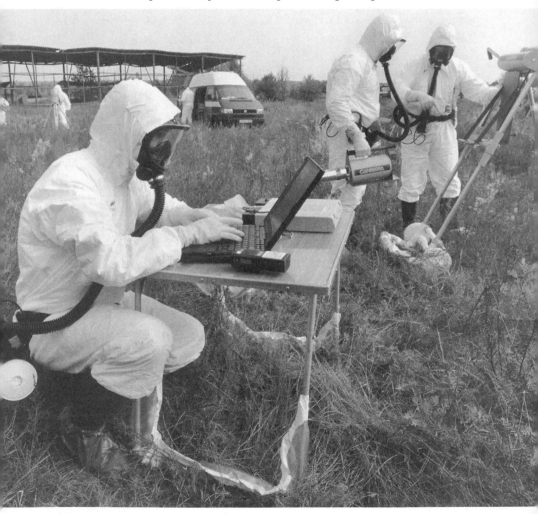

down the reaction. And the Soviet reactor was not contained, as it was at Three Mile Island.

In spite of these two accidents, many countries continue to rely on nuclear power. France, for example, produces about 75 percent of its power from nuclear energy and plans to build more nuclear plants. The government of West Germany, however, has announced that it will phase out nuclear power. In the United States, public opposition to nuclear power remains strong.

In addition to fear of a catastrophe, there are other problems with nuclear power. Used fuel rods (which contain uranium) remain radioactive, although at low levels. Right now the United States has no place for these to be permanently stored. Efforts by the federal government to build a repository for these rods inside a mountain at Yucca, Nevada, have met intense opposition from Nevada residents. So instead, used fuel rods remain scattered in temporary locations around the country. Also, there is concern that terrorists may steal the plutonium produced by nuclear plants and use it to produce a bomb.

Cost alone poses a major disadvantage. The last nuclear power plant to start operations was Watts Bar in 1996, located in Tennessee. This plant was under construction for twenty-three years and cost billions of dollars more than projected. Some of this lengthy construction reflects the extensive amount of safety review required by current regulations, as well as protests by organizations opposed to nuclear power. Whatever the reason, companies cannot build many plants that do not come on line in time, and that exceed their budgets by vast amounts.

All in all, the future of nuclear power is highly uncertain. Its strongest feature at the moment is the fact that it does not produce carbon dioxide and therefore cannot contribute to global warming. "As the world moves forward with emissions limits to reduce global warming, there is some renewed interest in nuclear power,"[37] notes Howard Geller, an energy expert who is trying to encourage a switch to renewable energy. But he does not think that nuclear technology will overcome the challenges it faces. And the Environmental Working Group, an activist organization, summarizes a widely held attitude toward nuclear power: "With its low emissions and low land use, nuclear [power] seems falsely attractive at first glance, but when you begin to look at its entire lifecycle, the potentially devastating human health and safety concerns are clear." [38]

Conclusion

Experts and citizens disagree over how severe the environmental impacts of various fuels are. Most of these impacts have declined over time, especially in developed countries such as the United States, and new technology is likely to continue to reduce them. But worry about the effects of radiation, air pollution, oil spills, and other effects remains a major factor in decisions about energy.

CHAPTER 4

Could Alternative Sources Replace Fossil Fuel?

I n mid-2003, Senator John Kerry, a candidate for the presidential nomination of the Democratic Party, sounded the theme of energy independence, arguing for greater reliance on domestic energy sources. "No foreign government can embargo clean, domestic, renewable sources of energy," he stated, "and no terrorist can seize control of them." [39] Kerry urged the development of wind and solar power. His message was that energy should come from domestic sources to the extent possible, but those sources should be environmentally attractive and renewable.

Kerry's emphasis on domestic energy sources resonated with many citizens. Indeed, President George W. Bush had already sounded a similar theme in his 2003 State of the Union speech. He promised "to promote energy independence for our country, while dramatically improving the environment." [40] One proposal was to add $1.2 billion more to the $500 million federal program to develop a car powered by hydrogen fuel cells. Bush estimated that a hydrogen-fueled car could be on the road by 2020.

Hydrogen is attractive because when it is burned it combines with oxygen and produces no pollutants—just water. The hydrogen-based fuel cell is "essentially a battery that does not need recharging," [41] according to a Princeton University professor, Dan Cahan. Fuel cells have the potential to replace the internal combustion engine, and hydrogen is the most abundant element on the planet.

Alternative Fuels—How Feasible?

But hydrogen cars are far in the future. For the immediate years ahead, many people deeply hope that fossil fuels can be replaced by other alternative energy sources. "We can't drill, dig and destroy our way to energy independence," says Carl Pope, executive director of the Sierra Club, an environmental group. "Instead," he writes, "Americans want a balanced approach that gives us quicker, cleaner, cheaper, safer solutions like energy-efficient technologies, renewable power like solar and wind, and responsible additions to supply." [42]

Alternative energy sources, often called renewable energy sources to distinguish them from nonrenewable fossil fuels, include hydrogen, geothermal (underground pools of steam), and biomass (plant material that can be burned, including corn and sugarcane). To most advocates of alternative energy, however, wind and solar are the most promising.

Solar and wind energy emit no air pollutants and produce no carbon dioxide. The great thing about the Sun and the wind is that they are free. But the fact that they are free does not mean that these sources of energy do not have their drawbacks, including environmental ones.

Solar Power

Solar power is "the epitome of the clean, sustainable energy technology," [43] writes Edward S. Cassedy, a retired professor of electrical engineering who has written a book about sustainable energy. Solar energy systems capture the Sun's rays, using them in two distinct ways. The sunlight may be used to heat air or water or it can be transformed into electricity by photovoltaic cells made of silicon that create an electric current.

Although the Sun can be an efficient source of heat, photovoltaic cells can capture only a small part of the Sun's energy. Thus, the production of electricity by photovoltaic cells is not very efficient. According to Steve Hester, technical director of the Solar Electric Power Association, most photovoltaic cells can convert between 8 and 18 percent of the sunlight they receive into elec-

This solar energy plant in Kleinwulkow, Germany, supplies power to forty-five area households.

tricity. When combined to form photovoltaic panels, however, more electricity is lost and the efficiency drops to around 11 or 12 percent.

Because of this inefficiency, plus the cost of batteries to store the energy that is produced, solar power is expensive. One obstacle for solar power is the fact that most of its cost is up front. That is, photovoltaic cells are costly to make. Once the system is in place, though, the fuel source (the Sun) itself is free (although the panels must be maintained). Even so, when all the costs of solar power are accounted for, it remains more expensive than power from most fuels. The U.S. Department of Energy has calculated the cost of various kinds of power plants that are in the planning stages (taking into account all costs, not just operating or construction costs). These calculations, supplied by the Energy Information Administration, show that solar energy plants designed to generate electricity on a large scale are the most expensive. Prices will range from 13.2 to 18.2 cents per kilowatt-hour, compared with those from fossil fuel plants, which are predicted to range between 4.5 and 9.6 cents per kilowatt-hour.

On the positive side, costs of solar energy have fallen by 75 percent since the 1980s and continue to go down. And some applications of solar energy are competitive today, especially solar calculators (which can run off of both sunlight and electric light). Electric fences can be operated by solar power, using a battery to store energy and dispense it overnight. A new housing development in Kingman, Arizona, will be powered mostly by solar energy.

Subsidies at the federal and state levels, however, have been necessary to build a significant market for solar power. The hope is that by expanding the market through subsidies, the cost per solar unit will gradually decline. The California Energy Commission, for example, offers rebates of up to nearly 50 percent of the purchase price of solar power systems used in people's homes. Subsidies are not limited to residential users. ChevronTexaco recently completed a five-hundred-kilowatt solar facility near Bakersfield, California, where photovoltaic panels provide electricity to operate the company's oil wells.

Costs of solar energy have fallen by 75 percent since the 1980s and continue to go down.

But solar energy has some other drawbacks. It produces power only when the Sun is shining and its output can vary depending on cloud cover, weather, dust, heat, and even bird droppings. Batteries must be used if solar cells are to provide continual power. Like car batteries, solar batteries are made of a variety of plastics and metals, some of which may be toxic. Solar batteries are expensive. And solar power plants require significant amounts of space, although individual units can be placed on roofs.

Solar power still does not supply more than 1 percent of energy in the United States. Even so, there are promising applications for the future. One will be in the rural areas of developing countries, where large electrical generation and transmission systems are missing and not likely to be built soon. Jack M. Hollander, author of *The Real Environmental Crisis,* says that more than 2 billion small solar units—even household based—could light and warm the homes of people who "lack even the basic energy services of electricity and heat."[44] He criticizes the governments of wealthy nations for concentrating so much on complex solar power technologies when they could be helping poorer countries with simpler solar power that he says is available now. Indeed, statistician Bjørn Lomborg reports that Sukatani, a village in Indonesia far from major urban centers, obtained electricity for the first time in 1989 through solar energy cells. The cells power lights and televisions and pump water from a well. In India, a school known as Barefoot College is spreading solar power to remote villages that have no electricity.

Wind Energy

Wind energy, the other alternative for which hopes are high, has been used for centuries. Windmills have accomplished a variety of tasks, such as grinding grain or pumping water. "The windmill, even more than the railroad, was crucial to settling the West,"[45] writes Stuart Leuthner in *Invention & Technology.* In the arid regions of the country they were used primarily to run pumps that lifted water from wells, and even today some are used for that purpose on ranches and farms.

Today wind energy is experiencing something of a rebirth, although, like solar energy, it still produces no more than 1 percent of the energy used in the United States. Today's electricity-producing windmill is usually a tall tower with a two- or three-blade propeller. The blades rotate in the wind, producing mechanical energy that is converted into electricity by a generator atop the tower. The size can range from small personal wind turbines attached to roofs to groups of giant windmills (as high as 160 feet and with blades as large as 130 feet wide) clustered together in wind farms. Electricity from wind farms is sold and transmitted to existing utility power grids, which deliver it to customers.

Wind farms such as this are often located in remote areas. The electricity such plants produce must be transported over great distances.

But wind energy, too, has economic and environmental problems. Breezes blow intermittently, so wind energy cannot provide energy consistently. Not only must the winds be strong enough to move the blades fast enough to power a turbine, but if the blades turn too fast, the windmill can be damaged, so windmills are designed to stop turning or slow down at higher wind speeds. Windmills must be a supplemental source, providing extra electricity to power grids rather than serving as the sole source of power.

Although wind is less expensive than solar power, it does not yet compete effectively with conventional sources such as coal or oil. One reason for its high cost is that most wind farms are in remote areas, and the electricity they produce must be carried a long distance on transmission lines. Another is that even large wind farms produce relatively small amounts of energy. According to Hollander, a wind farm would require about seventeen thousand acres of land to produce the amount of energy that a typical nuclear power plant produces. "The main reason wind is taking off now is the huge financial incentive provided by government subsidies,"[46] says Katharine Q. Seelye, writing in the *New York Times* in 2003.

Even some longtime advocates of wind energy are having second thoughts about it. Windmills are big, often loud, and their twirling blades can kill birds. Some people think that they are eyesores. And windy sites may be just the kind of scenic place that environmentalists do not want to disturb. Robert F. Kennedy Jr., a proponent of wind power, was dismayed to learn about plans for large turbines off the shore of Cape Cod, where his grandparents have a summer home. "There are appropriate places for everything,"[47] he says, and the Massachusetts coastline is not one of them.

Many environmentalists still favor wind energy over other alternatives, however. The Environmental Working Group writes: "Once installed, turbines produce no air or water pollution beyond a negligible amount produced during occasional maintenance."[48] The windmills' trade association, the American Wind Energy Association, contends that careful placement and installation of wind farms can avoid problems with noise or unsightliness. The National Audubon Society persuaded a wind farm developer to move a proposed wind farm near Los Angeles away from the migratory flight path of the California condor, an endangered bird.

Hydroelectric Power

Hydroelectric power is also a clean source of power; that is, it emits no pollutants and is often considered an alternative energy source. Yet hydropower, too, has become a subject of contention.

Dams convert rivers into lakes. Fast-moving water from the lakes spins turbines that generate electricity. Unlike wind or solar energy, large hydroelectric plants provide a constant source of energy.

How much countries rely on water power depends on the quantity and size of their rivers, the demand for electricity, and the costs of other sources. Hydropower produces only about 7 percent of the electricity in the United States, yet it provides two-thirds of Canada's electricity, ninety percent of Brazil's electricity, and almost all of Norway's and Zambia's electricity. In all, about 20 percent of the world's electricity is hydroelectric power, according to retired engineering professor Edward S. Cassedy.

Power-producing dams have been widely used in the developing world, often with financial support from the World Bank, an international development organization supported by the industrialized countries. Yet many people are understandably opposed to the widespread building of dams because they often force massive dislocations of people. The World Bank "provided funding for thirty-two projects that expelled at least 600,000 Indians from their homes,"[49] writes Matthew Brown in an article on World Bank projects in India. (Not all of these projects were for power, however; some were built to control flooding.) The Chinese government is evacuating 1.3 million people because two cities and more than thirteen hundred villages lie in the path of the Three Gorges Dam on the Yangtze River. The goals of the $24 billion project are both electricity production and flood control.

In the United States many rivers have been subdued by dams, but most of these dams were built in relatively unpopulated areas, and there were no massive relocations. In addition to power, they provide irrigation water and create large reservoirs that are used for recreation and drinking water. But the dams do have environmental impacts.

They change rivers' ecosystems, flooding natural river valleys and reducing the water flow below the dam, sometimes to a trickle. One controversial dam, Glen Canyon Dam in northern Arizona, drowned a canyon that is said to have rivaled the Grand Canyon in beauty. In fact, some environmentalists are campaigning to breach or remove dams such as Glen Canyon.

Dams also harm fish. In California and the Pacific Northwest, some salmon subspecies have been declared endangered partly because dams inhibit their ability to swim to and from the ocean. The Bonneville Power Authority (BPA), which owns many dams in the Pacific Northwest, and other government agencies such as the U.S. Fish and Wildlife Service have spent nearly $3 billion attempting to help fish get past the dams to reach the ocean or to return to rivers to spawn. The BPA has installed fish ladders and even transported fish around dams in barges and trucks, yet some

Hydroelectric dams provide a constant source of energy and are nonpolluting. However, the dams alter the ecosystems of rivers and cause harm to fish.

salmon populations remain endangered. So although hydropower has its environmental attractions, its disturbance of the natural environment leads many to oppose it.

Other Alternatives

There are other alternative energy sources, too. Geothermal energy, for example, is energy from naturally occurring underground reservoirs of hot water and steam. In places where such pools exist near the surface, hot water can be piped to homes and businesses. In Klamath Falls, Oregon, geothermal water heats roads and sidewalks to reduce ice in winter. Geothermal steam, which can be a mile or more underground, can be used to fuel generators to produce electricity. Reykjavik, the capital of Iceland, uses geothermal energy for direct heating as well as for producing electricity.

Perhaps the most intriguing examples of alternative energy are small innovations that may someday prove significant on a wider scale. ConAgra, the large agricultural firm that produces Butterball turkeys, has started to turn its turkey waste into salable products—oil and gas. A firm called Changing World Technologies of Philadelphia developed a process called thermal depolymerization (TDP) that will transform 1.3 million gallons of turkey grease, fat, feathers, and entrails per day into oil, gas, and minerals. "If the TDP process works as anticipated, the possibilities are staggering," writes Linda Platts, a researcher who seeks out environmental innovations. She notes that if all U.S. agricultural waste could be processed "it would yield the equivalent of 4 billion gallons of oil a year."[50] It should be added, however, that companies who convert poultry waste into energy benefit from the same subsidy that is spurring investment in wind farms.

Sea Solar Power International is attempting to create electricity by taking advantage of the differences in ocean water temperatures in tropical zones. Using a technology called ocean thermal energy conversion, this company is attempting to use the varying temperatures of water to power turbines, thus producing electricity. The technology also allows the company to produce fresh water as a byproduct.

Although the future of these examples is unknown, they illustrate that entrepreneurs, spurred by both environmental benefits and the hope of profits, continue to explore new energy frontiers.

Environmentalists want the use of all fuels to be reduced through a less wasteful lifestyle.

Conservation

There is another important alternative—conservation. Reducing use of all fuels has been a goal of the environmental movement for many years. "The case for conservation is compelling," writes Denis Hayes, one of the organizers of the first Earth Day, in 1977. He insists that conservation does not have to mean living in a cold house but, rather, in a "well-insulated house with an efficient heating system." Conservation does not have to mean giving up automobiles, but can mean, instead, "trading in a seven-mile per-gallon status symbol for a forty-mile per-gallon commuter vehicle." Conservation "merely requires the curtailment of energy waste."[51] Thirty-four years later, President George W. Bush said virtually the same thing: "Conservation does not mean doing without. Thanks to new technology, it can mean doing better and smarter and cheaper."[52]

Indeed, after prices of energy rose in the 1970s, conservation—both voluntary and mandatory—kicked in. To save money people bought more fuel-efficient cars and insulated their homes, and businesses developed more efficient heating and cooling systems. At the same time Congress required cars to get more mileage per gallon, established standards for appliances to ensure that they did not waste energy, and subsidized energy audits of people's homes so they could learn how to insulate them and save fuel.

> Much of the nation's increasing use of energy reflects growth in population, not increases in consumption by the individual.

Fuel consumption went down temporarily. As economic growth continued and population grew, energy use went up again and continues to do so. But much of the nation's increasing use of energy reflects growth in population, not increases in consumption by the individual. According to the Energy Information Administration, when expenditures on energy are measured as a percent of the national income, energy expenditures have gone down substantially since 1981. In other words, Americans are spending less of their total income on energy than they used to.

Many people want to see more conservation—to reduce dependence on foreign oil and to reduce the environmental effects of fuels. Daniel Chiras, a professor of environmental policy and author of numerous books about the environment, has come up with steps that he thinks individuals should take to save energy. They include installing insulation, caulking and weather-stripping, buying energy-efficient appliances, limiting inside temperatures to seventy-eight degrees Fahrenheit in the summer and sixty-eight degrees Fahrenheit in the winter—turning out lights, living close to work, and doing more biking and walking. Chiras and others also recommend government mandates such as higher taxes on fuel, special taxes for "gas guzzlers" (vehicles that use too much gasoline per mile), and higher efficiency standards for appliances and cars.

Is Progress Too Slow?

Many of the renewable fuels have been talked about for decades, and conservation has been adopted in a number of areas, yet the United States still relies mostly on the traditional fuels—coal, oil, and natural gas. Economics helps explain why.

As long as fossil fuels are cheap, people have little incentive to spend more money on other fuels, unless those fuels offer a better value or service. These may be small niches such as solar-powered homes or geographical areas where fossil fuels are not easily obtained. But it is unrealistic to expect large applications of alternative fuels while fossil fuels are readily available at a reasonable price.

Those costs may be rising, however. Certainly, natural gas prices went up in 2003 and drivers paid two dollars per gallon for gasoline.

In 2003, some Americans paid more than two dollars per gallon for gasoline. Conservationists hope that rising prices will decrease dependence on fossil fuels.

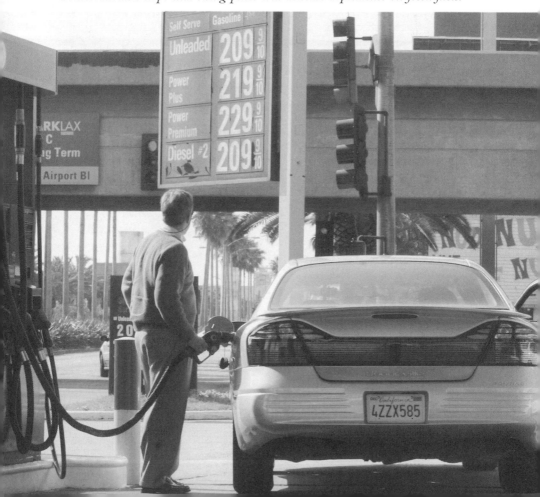

"It is no longer possible to meet the world demand for $20 oil, or the North American demand for $2.50 [natural] gas," a well-known forecaster, Henry Groppe, told an oil and gas industry group. The world is not awash in oil the way it was some years ago, he said. "The balance is so tight we could see rapidly rising oil prices." [53]

Whether those prices will be high enough to bring on alternative fuels is an unanswerable question. Today people may complain about a two-dollar gallon of gasoline, but Americans are so prosperous in the early twenty-first century that most can easily pay such prices. If prices begin to put strong pressure on people's pocketbooks, however, and if alternative fuel prices keep going down, new opportunities may emerge for the alternatives. And certainly higher prices will continue to boost conservation.

Conclusion

Every energy source has advantages and drawbacks. Even the most optimistic advocates for renewables like wind or solar energy recognize that each is likely to contribute only a portion of a multi-faceted energy future, yet those portions of the overall energy mix may be extremely important. The obstacles to widespread use of alternatives in wealthy countries—including their environmental flaws—are substantial; some analysts contend that fossil fuels will win out for many decades by becoming increasingly friendly to the environment. In sum, future energy choices are difficult to predict.

CHAPTER 5

How Does the Government Influence Energy Use?

The United States is largely a free-market country in which consumers and producers, not governmental officials, make most of the economic decisions. Yet actions by the federal government affect many of those decisions. Energy is no exception.

One important contribution is through funding research and development. Congress appropriates money to be funneled by the Department of Energy into a variety of projects. The department was created in 1977, largely in response to the oil embargo of 1973. Its major goal was to encourage energy independence by fostering new technologies that would stretch domestic fuels. In recent years its emphasis has been on promoting alternative fuels such as hydrogen fuel cells, wind energy, and solar power, as well as energy efficiency.

The federal government funds about a third of the nation's research and development in energy (the private sector funds the rest). Between 1978, the first full year of operation of the Department of Energy, and 1999 the government spent $91.5 billion on energy research and development. The department conducts long-range "blue sky" projects that the private sector is unlikely to pursue on its own and works in partnership with industry on practical improvements. One of its first major projects was attempting to liquefy coal. The goal was to combine it with hydrogen, remove

It would have been nice to know the pipes had broken while you were at the office.

President George W. Bush learns about some of the latest energy conservation technologies at the Department of Energy.

its impurities, and turn it into a liquid, which is easier to handle. Although work continues on liquefied coal, it is not viewed as a likely source of energy in the near future. The department also developed enhanced recovery techniques that helped oil companies pump more oil out of wells.

More recently the department has worked with major U.S. automakers and their suppliers to improve automobiles' fuel efficiency. In 1993 the program set a goal of developing a car that gets eighty miles to the gallon while meeting EPA standards for tailpipe emissions. (It has not quite reached that goal, but vehicles with very high mileage are near production.) If the eighty-mile-per-gallon goal is achieved, the car will probably be a hybrid that combines an electric battery and a small gasoline-powered internal combustion engine. The gasoline engine charges the battery as the car moves on electric power. (Some hybrids are already on the market.) For the longer term, the Department of Energy works with auto manufacturers on the hydrogen fuel cell as a possible complete replacement for the internal combustion engine.

Some of the federal government's research is very down-to-earth. In cooperation with appliance makers, it has helped develop refrigerators that use less energy. The refrigerator is the largest user of electricity in most homes, and today's refrigerators use less than one-third of the electricity that they required in 1974, even though they are typically much larger. The department also is working with General Electric and other lighting companies to reduce the costs of long-lasting compact fluorescent lightbulbs, which save energy. And it is collaborating with the metalworking and glassmaking industries to develop more efficient manufacturing processes.

Funding research is not the only way that the government attempts to address energy problems, of course. Congress often attempts to spur conservation through subsidies such as tax credits and exemptions, which are available to individuals and to corporations. There are two arguments for subsidizing solar and other alternative energy sources through taxpayer funds. One is that by expanding the market for these products, economies of scale will develop, lowering the costs of individual units such as photovoltaic modules or windmill towers. Eventually these products may be competitive on their own.

But the second reason is that even if solar and other renewables are more expensive, their environmental advantages may make them worth the price. Howard Geller argues that if all the "environmental and social costs" of fossil fuels could be measured and incorporated into the price, the price of fossil fuels would be higher than the prices of alternatives; that is, alternatives would be "the least-cost option."[54]

> Even if solar and other renewables are more expensive, their environmental advantages may make them worth the price.

To spur renewables, Congress provides a 10 percent credit on taxes of companies that invest in solar or geothermal equipment. It allows producers of wind energy to reduce their taxes by 1.5 cents for every kilowatt-hour of power they produce. It exempts producers of fuels that include ethanol (a fuel additive made from bio-

This married couple lives in a sod-covered, solar-powered home in California. Using solar energy entitles the couple to a generous tax credit.

mass, usually corn) from part of the federal excise tax on gasoline—
5.2 cents per gallon. It helps homeowners obtain lower-cost mort-
gages for energy-efficient homes.

These subsidies are not universally endorsed, however. Some
critics point out that nearly every form of energy gets some kind
of special treatment, regardless of the benefits to the public. For
example, even though enthusiasm for renewables is high, Congress
still supports conventional energy. A law enacted by Congress in
1957, the Price-Anderson Act, protects nuclear power companies
by limiting their liability for payment of damages in the case of a
terrible nuclear accident. That is, if the companies had to com-
pensate victims of the accident, they would be able to draw on the
resources of the federal government for financial help. For many
years, the oil industry received a special favor from the government; a large tax deduction known as the oil depletion allowance.
Such benefits helped traditional energy sources keep a strong
foothold.

And when it comes to alternative energy, some kinds of renewables fare better than others. Ethanol, produced from corn,
received about $1 billion in state and federal subsidies each year
between 1979 and 2000 according to the General Accounting
Office. (The states where corn is a major agricultural crop also
subsidize ethanol.) According to the Renewable Energy Policy
Project, a nonprofit organization that promotes alternative fuels, however solar energy has received a total of $4.4 billion and
wind energy $1.3 billion, small in comparison to ethanol's sup-
port.

Indeed, the motivation behind congressionally mandated subsidies is sometimes questionable. The chance to obtain favors from
what is called the political pork barrel may drive subsidies as much
as public policy goals. In 2003 environmentalist Carl Pope of the
Sierra Club and Edward H. Crane, head of the Cato Institute, a
free market advocacy group, together wrote an article in the *Washington Post* expressing their disgust with the energy pork barrel.
They jointly chastised Congress for the two energy bills that were
under consideration. One of the bills, they said, had "$33 billion
in tax breaks and subsidies, the great majority of which are awarded
to the coal, oil, and nuclear industries." The competing bill had "a

hurricane of subsidies, tax breaks, and regulatory preferences for every energy industry you can imagine."[55] Pope and Crane argued that the subsidies wasted taxpayer money by propping up energy companies that have political clout. They argued that it would be better to drop all the subsidies and create a "level playing field" in which renewables and fossil fuels both took their chances in the marketplace.

Laws affecting energy sometimes have unintended consequences. This can happen when the requirements of the law conflict with the goals of individuals and corporations, who may figure out ways to get around them. Their actions may cause unexpected results, and the laws may not even achieve the goals that motivated Congress in the first place. One illustration of the complex results of federal laws is the nation's fuel-efficiency standards.

Miles-per-Gallon Regulation

Today's cars look, feel, and operate as they do partly because of government-mandated Corporate Average Fuel Economy (CAFE) standards. These fuel-efficiency standards go back to 1975 and reflect Congress's desire to reduce Americans' dependence on foreign oil by requiring auto manufacturers to design cars to go farther on a gallon of gasoline.

Before 1975 auto manufacturers were not forced to produce cars that met specific fuel-economy standards. They could make cars with whatever mileage per gallon they wanted to. The automakers' chief goal was to appeal to the consumer. And with gasoline relatively cheap during the 1960s, not very many people placed a high priority on fuel-efficient cars. After OPEC's oil embargo of 1973, however, consumers began to demand better mileage.

Congress, too, wanted better mileage, and in 1975 it told automakers that they had to bring their vehicles up to an average of 18 miles per gallon for cars and to 15.8 miles per gallon for light trucks. (Miles per gallon could vary for different makes of vehicle, but the standards set the average for a company's entire fleet.) This was a big leap because on average, cars achieved slightly more than 13 miles per gallon at the time. Like the 55-mile-per-hour speed limit (enacted about the same time), the CAFE law was designed to save fuel and make Americans more energy independent.

Currently, CAFE standards are 27.5 miles per gallon for cars and 20.7 miles per gallon for light trucks, and some people are urging Congress to raise them even more—as high as 40 miles per gallon. Automakers have objected to the standards every step of the way, but have generally been able to meet them.

Did the higher mileage-per-gallon standards achieve what Congress wanted? To some extent, yes. A 2002 report of the National Research Council concluded that the CAFE standards did have an impact, although not much at first. According to the council, higher oil prices in the 1970s spurred the automakers to improve their fuel efficiency anyway, simply to maintain sales. The standards merely "reinforced" this trend. Later, however, the standards were "particularly effective in keeping fuel economy above the levels to which it might have fallen when real gasoline prices began their long decline in the early 1980s." [56]

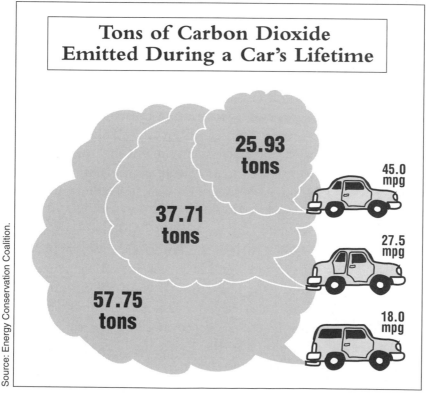

Tons of Carbon Dioxide Emitted During a Car's Lifetime

25.93 tons — 45.0 mpg

37.71 tons — 27.5 mpg

57.75 tons — 18.0 mpg

Source: Energy Conservation Coalition.

The standards, however, did not actually reduce the imports of oil. Imports represented 35 percent of all the oil consumed in the United States in 1974; by 2002 that figure had risen to more than 52 percent. One reason that dependence on imported oil kept growing was that people drove more. They "drive twice as many miles as they did when CAFE was enacted,"[57] says H. Sterling Burnett of the National Center for Policy Analysis. When it is possible to drive farther on a gallon of gasoline, many people do just that. They drive more, eating up the fuel savings.

The CAFE standards also had an unintended consequence—a detrimental effect on safety. In order to meet the standards, automakers made many technical changes, such as redesigning transmissions and fuel-injection systems. But according to Robert Crandall and John D. Graham, who conducted an extensive study of the standards, the biggest single factor in achieving the CAFE standards was reducing the weight of cars. Manufacturers made cars smaller, reshaped them, and used lighter-weight materials.

Lighter cars are not as safe as heavier cars. People riding in a small car are more likely to die when their car crashes into another car or smashes against a tree or barrier. The 2001 National Research Council study acknowledged that CAFE standards contribute to between thirteen hundred and twenty-six hundred additional deaths each year (although two members of the council writing the report expressed doubt about those numbers). "Too many people have already been sacrificed at the altar of 'fuel efficiency,'" says James M. Taylor, managing editor of *Environment & Climate News,* a publication that is critical of government regulations. "Further raising CAFE standards would kill additional thousands of innocent people each year."[58]

Companies also found a way around the CAFE standards. Sport utility vehicles, or SUVs, such as the Ford Excursion, the GMC Yukon, and the Jeep Grand Cherokee are considered "light trucks," and therefore can meet the lower CAFE standards. Automakers recognized that many Americans were dissatisfied with the lighter and smaller but fuel-efficient passenger cars. So when the price of gasoline began to go down in the 1980s, they began to modify their light trucks in order to appeal to passenger markets and SUVs were born.

Critics of sports utility vehicles condemn the vehicles for their fuel inefficiency and high emissions.

At the time of CAFE's enactment, light trucks were mostly vehicles for hauling goods, and they represented only about 20 percent of the total vehicle market. Today they make up almost 50 percent of the market.

But SUVs are under attack. First, they are less fuel efficient than traditional cars; they were developed in part to avoid the CAFE limitations. Second, as light trucks, they do not have to meet pollution control standards as tough as those affecting other passenger cars. Because of their heavier weight, they are generally safer for the occupants when accidents occur, but they pose a greater risk for smaller cars they may collide with. And some models are more likely to roll over on curves. In addition, SUVs can be large

and intimidating to other drivers, and some people react to them
as symbols of Americans' complacency and wealth. After observ-
ing SUVs crowding the parking lot at his child's middle school,
writer Gregg Easterbrook said, "These vehicles have converted driving from a convenience and sometimes a pleasure into a nerve-
wracking Darwinian battle." [59]

The experience of CAFE illustrates how government regulation may respond to a public problem but cause problems of its
own. In this case, the desire for energy independence led to changes
in the kinds of cars that consumers buy. It is not clear that it had
an appreciable effect on energy independence. Partly because Americans drove more, imports of petroleum went up, not down. The
standards also led to a great deal of wasted time and money, as companies first lobbied against the regulations and then devised ways
around them.

In spite of these drawbacks, raising fuel-economy standards is
extremely popular. Many people think that if the standards are high
enough, they will encourage energy independence. Energy expert
Howard Geller estimates that the auto companies could achieve
forty-four miles per gallon for cars and thirty-three miles per gallon for light trucks by 2012, and he contends that meeting these
standards would save at least 1 million barrels of petroleum per day.

Strange Coalitions

As the CAFE standards indicate, laws can be manipulated by politicians and special interest lobbyists, and this is especially likely when
profits and losses depend on how laws are written or interpreted.
Robert L. Bradley Jr., energy analyst and author of a two-volume
history, *Oil, Gas & Government: The U.S. Experience,* says that government intervention "is rarely enacted by legislators looking out
for the general public over the objections of business," as most people suppose. Rather, he says, it is generally "enacted by identifiable
coalitions of business firms and politicians." [60] In the case of CAFE,
the separate standards for cars and light trucks presented a loop-
hole that companies took advantage of. Responding to consumers,
manufacturers figured out how to avoid making all their vehicles
as fuel efficient as Congress had hoped.

Environmental groups have had a major role in determining the
environmental laws that affect energy. But they, too, have been

caught up in the political process, so the outcome of the laws they champion is not always what they had hoped. An illustration of this is a now-famous coalition that helped shape the Clean Air Act Amendments of 1977.

In the mid-1970s, the new environmental movement was showing its muscle. One of its key goals was to persuade Congress to force electric power plants to reduce their smokestack emissions of sulfur dioxide. At the time, power plants could lower their emissions in one of two ways. They could switch to low-sulfur coal, which would send less sulfur into the atmosphere when the coal was burned, or they could burn high-sulfur coal but also install large, expensive devices called scrubbers (one in Ohio cost $800 million) that chemically remove sulfur from the smokestack emissions.

Buying low-sulfur coal—even if it meant transporting coal from distant locations in the western United States—was much cheaper than installing scrubbers in new plants. But coal producers in Appalachian states such as West Virginia and Kentucky, supported by strong coal miners' unions, did not want electric power plants to meet the regulations this way. A lot of the coal in Appalachia is high in sulfur. The companies would have lost important markets for their coal if electric utilities switched to low-sulfur coal. So,

The outcome of the laws [environmental groups] champion is not always what they had hoped.

aided by powerful legislators, coal producers lobbied Congress to require that electric utilities add scrubbers—and they won.

Once scrubbers became mandatory, utilities could not save money by using low-sulfur coal. They had to put the scrubbers in anyway, so they might as well use the high-sulfur coal, especially if it were nearby. The sulfur-removing devices did not even work very well if the coal was too low in sulfur.

Bruce Ackerman and William T. Hassler, who studied the history of this legislation, see the environmentalists as pawns of the coal companies. Environmentalists were eager to force the utilities to stop polluting and did not care whether scrubbers or low-sulfur coal was used (although they preferred scrubbers because that made certain that *something* was being done). The high-sulfur coal lobbyists manipulated the environmentalists' concern to promote legislation that forced utilities to buy high-sulfur coal. With the passage of the 1977 Clean Air Act Amendments, some improvement in the environment did occur. But the price was high because scrubbers were so costly. Furthermore, Ackerman and Hassler think that the air ended up dirtier than if the government had allowed the purchase of low-sulfur coal. The scrubbers were a new and untested technology and difficult to use.

Fortunately this situation only lasted until 1990. Then Congress passed amendments to the Clean Air Act that removed the requirement for scrubbers but insisted on even greater reductions in sulfur emissions.

Deregulation

In recent years the government's role in energy has been changing in two important areas: electricity production and natural gas. Governments regulate these two industries. They limit the prices that the producers can charge customers, and they set rules and regulations about how they conduct their businesses. The sale of electricity and natural gas to retail customers such as homes and businesses is regulated primarily by state governments, whereas the transmission of electricity and the transport of natural gas across state lines must be approved by the Federal Energy Regulatory Commission.

The reason for this direct regulation is that electricity and natural gas were originally considered to be natural monopolies. Economists use the term *monopoly* to indicate a company that has a lot of power over its customers because a competitive market does not exist. A company has a natural monopoly if the nature of the product it sells prevents competition from developing.

Economists have viewed the sale of natural gas and electricity as a natural monopoly because transmitting gas and electricity involves a massive network of pipelines or wires reaching from a natural gas field or an electric utility to individual homes and offices. The cost of building this network of pipes or wires is very high—so high, in fact, that once the system is in place, other companies

Due to the high cost of building transmission networks, electricity was originally considered to be a natural monopoly.

are not likely to come in and build another one, bringing competition to the customers. "The duplication of facilities would cost more than the benefits of competition would be worth," explains David Howard Davis. "To substitute for the hidden hand of competition, government feels it must regulate the utility to be sure that the consumers enjoy the savings and that the greater efficiency does not merely enrich the company." [61]

In recent years, however, economists have reconsidered this concept of natural monopoly. After all, even though two natural gas companies are not likely to compete for a single homeowner's business, consumers do have energy choices. For example, they can heat their homes with electricity, natural gas, and even fuel oil. The market is not as monopolistic as economists used to think.

Because of this rethinking, and for other reasons such as new technology, a new concept developed in both the natural gas and electricity markets—deregulation. Starting in the late 1980s, federal and state governments began to loosen up their rules and regulations. They did not drop all control, but they allowed companies more freedom. For example, the federal government allowed producers to purchase electricity from plants located hundreds of miles away. If it is hot in San Francisco, if air conditioners were humming and the demand for electricity is high, a utility can purchase electricity from a place that has unused electricity such as Seattle, and send it along the transmission wires to San Francisco. The utilities involved can negotiate their own prices for this "wheeled-in" electricity.

Partial deregulation was a factor behind the sudden 2003 blackout that traveled across the northeastern United States and part of Canada.

But regulation of prices to the consumer remains under the control of state commissions. And these commissions, which face a lot of pressure from the public when energy prices rise, have not wanted to let the prices rise very far. One reason behind the shortage of electricity in California in 2001 was the fact that consumers were not paying the full cost of electricity. When the suppliers of electricity suddenly faced extremely high prices, the utilities were caught in a squeeze between high costs and low revenues. One utility, the Pacific Gas and Electric Company, went bankrupt.

Similarly, partial deregulation was a factor behind the sudden 2003 blackout that traveled across the northeastern United States and part of Canada. Companies had used the freedom of deregulation to invest in producing more electricity, but transmission lines were still largely regulated, and sometimes the government would require companies to open up their transmission lines without compensation. Companies declined to invest a lot in transmission. According to the *Wall Street Journal,* demand for electricity has increased by about 35 percent over the past ten years, but the transmission system grew by only about 18 percent.

But the blackout was a wake-up call, and it is likely that serious changes will be made. Whether the trend will be toward more regulation or more deregulation is hard to say.

New Yorkers walk across the Brooklyn Bridge from Manhattan during the 2003 blackout. Incomplete deregulation of energy markets contributed to the blackout.

Conclusion

The federal government has multiple roles that affect how energy is produced and used. The goals of government intervention vary depending on changing conditions and political pressures. In considering the appropriate role for government in the energy field, perhaps the most important lesson to draw from them is that intervention has pitfalls as well as promises.

Thinking Critically About the Future

A s the twenty-first century begins, Americans are torn by two conflicting motives when it comes to energy: They want secure energy, and they want to protect their environment. As a result they want to reduce reliance on fossil fuels, because so much oil is imported and because fossil fuels have substantial environmental impacts.

At the same time, fossil fuels remain plentiful. Prices, although sometimes high, appear to be well within the budgets of most Americans. Few people and few companies are motivated to seek out different fuels for the short term.

And even if alternative renewable fuels were competitive in price, the evidence suggests that there is no single "environmentally correct" fuel. All fuels have their strengths and their weaknesses. Perhaps the most that can be said confidently about energy in the next decade is that alternative fuels are likely to find some new markets, but no one knows how large they will be. Certainly conventional fuels will stay in the mix.

Meanwhile, increasing efforts, supported by the federal government as well as industry, to develop renewable sources of power will undoubtedly characterize the years ahead. Wind, solar, hydropower, and even more exotic fuels will continue to be subject to intense development, sometimes at taxpayer expense.

One of the ironies of the push toward cleaner fuels is that it has put pressure on the cleanest of the fossil fuels—natural gas. Most power plants in the planning stages will use natural gas rather than coal. This switch to natural gas puts pressure on the federal government to open up more areas for drilling in the West. This pressure runs into conflict with many environmentalists, as well as some local residents. Rising natural gas prices may even turn Americans to foreign sources of energy again, this time to liquefied natural gas, which is natural gas that has been compressed so that it can be carried by tankers.

On the positive side, Americans can take a great deal of satisfaction from the fact that fuels are cleaner than they used to be, and that environmental quality is improving. Even when it comes to

Steve Schneider, CEO of Zero Air Pollution (ZAP), sits in the prototype of a ZAP electric car that produces no emissions.

dependence on foreign oil, there is some positive news. The advent of the hybrid car, fueled by an electric battery that is constantly recharged with a gasoline-powered engine, offers hope for gradually replacing the traditional internal combustion engine. And a hydrogen fuel cell is a possibility for the distant future.

No one can predict the future. If current trends continue, there is reason for both concern and hope, but not all is somber in the world of energy.

Notes

Chapter 1: Are We Running Out of Energy?

1. Susan Warren and Melanie Trottman, "Getting Unplugged Sheds Light on What Is Wired These Days," *Wall Street Journal,* August 18, 2003, p. A1.

2. Quoted in Matt Richtel, "Coping Without Electricity in California E-World," *New York Times,* January 28, 2001. www.ny times.com.

3. Todd S. Purdum, "California Power Crisis Replays a Familiar Theme," *New York Times,* January 25, 2001. www.nytimes.com.

4. David Howard Davis, *Energy Politics.* New York: St. Martin's, 1974, p. 1.

5. Benjamin Zycher, "OPEC," *Concise Encyclopedia of Economics,* Library of Economics and Liberty, 2003. www.econlib. org.

6. Donella H. Meadows, et al., *The Limits to Growth: A Report for the Club of Rome's Project on the Predicament of Mankind.* New York: Universe Books, 1972, p. 23.

7. *Newsweek,* "Running Out of Everything," November 19, 1973.

8. *Newsweek,* "Oil Prices Hit the Skids," January 24, 1983.

9. John U. Nef, "An Early Energy Crisis and Its Consequences," *Scientific American,* November 1977, p. 141.

10. F.D. Ommanney, *Lost Leviathan.* New York: Dodd, Mead, 1971, p. 92.

11. Bjørn Lomborg, *The Skeptical Environmentalist: Measuring the Real State of the World.* New York: Cambridge University Press, 2001, pp. 121–22.

12. Paul R. Ehrlich and Anne H. Ehrlich, *Healing the Planet.* Boston, MA: Addison-Wesley, 1991, p. 13.

13. Ehrlich and Ehrlich, *Healing the Planet,* p. 11.

Chapter 2: Should Public Lands Be Opened to Energy Development?

14. James E. Mielke, "Oil in the Ocean: The Short- and Long-Term Impacts of a Spill," Congressional Research Service Report No. 90-356 SPR, Library of Congress, July 24, 1990.

15. Arctic Refuge Science Letter Signatories, letter to President George W. Bush, March 20, 2001. www.defenders.org.

16. Quoted in Tom Kenworthy, "Study Condemns Arctic Oil Drilling," *Washington Post,* August 27, 1995, p. A4.

17. Defenders of Wildlife, cartoon video. www.savearcticrefuge.org.

18. Jack Lentfer, written testimony for House Committee on Resources Hearing on Republican Energy Bill "Energy Security Act," July 11, 2001.

19. Steven Amstrup, personal communication with author, September 29, 2003.

20. Robert H. Nelson, "A Frigid Eden," *Forbes,* April 24, 1995, p. 122.

21. William H. Meadows, "Arctic Refuge: Key to Saving Wild America," in Subhankar Banerjee, ed., *Arctic National Wildlife Refuge: Seasons of Life and Land.* Seattle, WA: Mountaineers Books, 2003, pp. 122, 126.

22. David Sibley, "Visiting the Birds at Their Summer Home," in Banerjee, *Arctic National Wildlife Refuge,* p. 109.

23. Benjamin P. Nageak, "Inupiat Eskimos First, Best Environmentalists." Energy Stewardship Alliance, June 30, 2003. www.anwr.org.

24. Quoted in Allanna Sullivan, "Fates of Alaska Tribes May Ride on Impact of Drilling in Refuge," *Wall Street Journal,* November 2, 1995, p. A6.

25. Quoted in Holly Lippke Fretwell, "Federal Estate: Is Bigger Better?" Public Lands Report III, Political Economy Research Center (PERC), 2000, p. 2.

26. Quoted in Robert Gehrke, "White House Wants to Speed Oil, Gas Drilling," *Bozeman Daily Chronicle,* August 10, 2003, p. A12.

27. Alan Greenspan, testimony before the U.S. Senate Committee on Energy and Natural Resources, July 10, 2003.

28. Reid Lea, "A Free Market Environmentalist Discovers He Is One," *PERC Reports,* Political Economy Research Center, August 1992, p. 7.

29. John Flicker, "Don't Desecrate the Arctic Refuge," *Wall Street Journal,* September 18, 1995, p. A19.

30. Flicker, "Don't Desecrate the Arctic Refuge," p. A19.

Chapter 3: How Harmful Are Current Energy Sources?

31. Jack M. Hollander, *The Real Environmental Crisis.* Berkeley: University of California Press, 2003, p. 140.

32. *Nature,* "Welcome to the Anthropocene," August 14, 2003, p. 709.

33. James E. Hansen et al., "Global Warming in the 21st Century: An Alternative Scenario," NASA Goddard Institute for Space Studies, April 17, 2001. www.giss.nasa.gov.

34. Quoted in Three Mile Island Alert, "It Was the First Step in a Nuclear Nightmare." www.tmia.com.

35. Merrill Sheils, "Nuclear Accident," *Newsweek,* April 9, 1979, p. 24.

36. Hollander, *The Real Environmental Crisis,* p. 157.

37. Howard Geller, *Energy Revolution: Policies for a Sustainable Future.* Washington, DC: Island Press, 2003, p. 26.

38. Environmental Working Group, "Sources of Electricity," 2003. www.ewg.org.

Chapter 4: Could Alternative Sources Replace Fossil Fuel?

39. Quoted in Dan Balz, "Kerry to Unveil Energy Independence Policy," *Washington Post,* June 13, 2003, p. 7.

40. George W. Bush, "State of the Union," White House: News, January 28, 2003. www.whitehouse.gov.

41. Dan Cahan, "What Is a Fuel Cell?" www.princeton.edu/~dcahan/fuelcells/index.shtml.

42. Carl Pope, "Sierra Club Urges Balanced Approach That's Quicker, Cleaner, Cheaper, Safer," Sierra Club, June 30, 2003. www.sierraclub.org.

43. Edward S. Cassedy, *Prospects for Sustainable Energy: A Critical Assessment*. New York: Cambridge University Press, 2000, p. 19.

44. Hollander, *The Real Environmental Crisis*, p. 153.

45. Stuart Leuthner, "The Windmills That Won the West," *Invention & Technology*, Fall 2003, p. 56.

46. Katharine Q. Seelye, "Windmills Sow Dissent for Environmentalists," *New York Times*, June 5, 2003, p. A28.

47. Quoted in Seelye, "Windmills Sow Dissent for Environmentalists," p. A28.

48. Environmental Working Group, "Sources of Electricity."

49. Matthew Brown, "Banking on Disaster: The World Bank and Environmental Destruction," in Donald R. Leal and Roger E. Meiners, eds., *Government vs. Environment*. Lanham, MD: Rowman & Littlefield, 2002, p. 147.

50. Linda Platts, "Garbage to Oil," *PERC Reports*, Political Economy Research Center, June 2003, p. 15.

51. Denis Hayes, *Rays of Hope*. New York: W.W. Norton, 1977, pp. 86-87.

52. George W. Bush, "Remarks by the President to Capital City Partnership," White House: News, May 17, 2001. www.whitehouse.gov.

53. Quoted in *American Oil & Gas Reporter*, "Analyst Predicts Higher Oil, Gas Prices," August 2003, p. 118.

Chapter 5: How Does the Government Influence Energy Use?

54. Geller, *Energy Revolution*, p. 56.

55. Edward H. Crane and Carl Pope, "Fueled by Pork," *Washington Post*, July 30, 2002. www.cato.org.

56. National Research Council, *Effectiveness and Impact of Corporate Average Fuel Economy (CAFE) Standards.* Washington, DC: National Academy of Sciences, 2002, p. 3.

57. H. Sterling Burnett, "CAFE's Three Strikes—It Should Be Out," Brief Analysis No. 388, National Center for Policy Analysis, February 13, 2002, p. 1.

58. James M. Taylor, "Time to Fight the CAFE Leviathan," *Environment & Climate News,* March 1, 2002. www.heartland.org.

59. Gregg Easterbrook, "Axle of Evil," *New Republic,* January 30, 2003, p. 27. www.tnr.com.

60. Robert L. Bradley Jr., *Oil, Gas & Government: The U.S. Experience.* Lanham, MD: Rowman & Littlefield, 1996, p. 1818.

61. Davis, *Energy Politics,* p. 116.

Glossary

biomass: Renewable organic matter such as wood, plants, and plant and animal waste.

British thermal unit (Btu): A measurement of energy, used to describe the energy content of a fuel (for example, a barrel of oil produces 5.8 million Btu).

carbon dioxide (CO_2): A trace gas in the atmosphere formed when carbon-containing fuels combine with oxygen in the air through combustion; it is believed to contribute to global warming.

crude oil: Unrefined liquid hydrocarbons found in underground reservoirs.

curie: A measurement of radioactivity.

electricity: An energy form in which charged particles move, creating a current.

electric utility: A private or public company that generates and distributes electrical energy to consumers.

emissions: Releases into the atmosphere.

fossil fuel: An energy source from decayed organic material that contains hydrocarbons and is formed in the earth's crust.

fuel cell: A device that generates electrical energy from a chemical reaction between hydrogen fuel and oxygen.

generator: A machine that converts mechanical energy into electrical energy.

geothermal energy: Energy in the form of hot water or steam that is found in reservoirs, usually deep in the earth.

global warming: Rising average world surface temperatures often attributed to increases in greenhouse gases.

hybrid car: A vehicle that is fueled by more than one source of energy.

hydrocarbon: An organic compound made up of only hydrogen and carbon.

hydroelectric power: Electrical energy created by water flowing through a turbine.

kilowatt–hour (kwh): A measure of electrical energy, equal to the energy produced when one thousand watts of power are used for one hour.

liquefied natural gas (LNG): Natural gas at a temperature low enough to make it a liquid so that it occupies less space.

monopoly: A company that has the ability to keep prices high because there is little or no competition in its market.

natural gas: A mixture of gaseous hydrocarbon compounds used for fuel.

natural monopoly: A company that can keep prices high because the nature of its products keeps out competition.

nitrogen oxide (NO_x): One of several gases composed of nitrogen and oxygen, created by the burning of fossil fuels.

nuclear reactor: A complicated device in which uranium atoms are split, energy produced, and the reaction controlled.

nuclear reactor core: The unit in which a nuclear reaction takes place.

petroleum: A class of liquid hydrocarbon mixtures including crude oil, gasoline, diesel, and others.

photovoltaic cell: A device that creates an electric current when the Sun shines on it.

photovoltaic module: Photovoltaic cells that are grouped together in a panel.

proven reserves: The estimated quantities of a resource that can be recovered in the future under current economic and operating conditions.

real price: The price of a good adjusted for change in the value of money over time.

solar energy: Energy in the Sun's rays that is captured either as heat or electrical energy.

subsidy: Funds or other benefits provided by the government.

sulfur dioxide (SO_2): An irritating, colorless gas created by the reaction of sulfur and oxygen.

transmission lines: The network of wires that carry energy from where it is generated to customers.

turbine: A machine that converts energy from a moving gas or liquid into mechanical energy that powers a generator.

watt: A basic measurement of electrical power.

wind energy: Mechanical or electrical energy captured or generated from moving air.

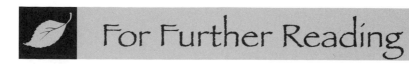 For Further Reading

Books

Edward S. Cassedy, *Prospects for Sustainable Energy: A Critical Assessment.* New York: Cambridge University Press, 2000. A detailed overview of alternative energy systems and how they work; suitable for serious students.

Paul R. Ehrlich and Anne H. Ehrlich, *Healing the Planet.* Boston, MA: Addison-Wesley, 1991. Two famous critics of current energy policies offer a broad range of arguments for changing today's energy and environmental choices.

Howard Geller, *Energy Revolution: Policies for a Sustainable Future.* Washington, DC: Island Press, 2003. A readable book that proposes many strategies for switching from fossil fuels not only in North America but around the world.

Jack M. Hollander, *The Real Environmental Crisis.* Berkeley: University of California Press, 2003. A careful reconsideration of many environmental issues, including energy, with the goal of encouraging policies that would improve the lives of people in the third world.

Bjørn Lomborg, *The Skeptical Environmentalist: Measuring the Real State of the World.* New York: Cambridge University Press, 2001. A former Greenpeace member shares why he is more optimistic about energy and the environment than he used to be.

Periodicals

Robert L. Bradley Jr., "The Increasing Sustainability of Conventional Energy," *Cato Policy Analysis No. 341.* Washington, DC: Cato Institute, April 22, 1999.

Gregg Easterbrook, "Axle of Evil," *New Republic,* January 30, 2003.

David Freedman, "Fuel Cells vs. the Grid," *Technology Review,* January/February, 2002.

Rebecca Smith, "Blackout Signals Major Weaknesses in U.S. Power Grid," *Wall Street Journal,* August 18, 2003.

Websites

American Petroleum Institute (http://api-ec.api.org). This organization of oil producers offers a variety of information about energy.

American Wind Energy Association (www.awea.org). Operated by companies in the wind energy business, this site answers questions about wind energy.

Cooler Heads Coalition (www.globalwarming.org). An organization that doubts the severity of global warming explains why.

Energy Information Administration (www.eia.doe.gov). This extremely comprehensive site sponsored by the Department of Energy provides detailed statistics about energy use and production.

Renewable Energy Policy Project (http://solstice.crest.org). Proponents of alternative energy discuss the benefits.

Union of Concerned Scientists (www.ucsusa.org). This organization opposes nuclear power, supports renewable energy, and offers information on other topics such as global warming.

World Nuclear Association (www.world-nuclear.org). Supporters of nuclear power offer their views and information about nuclear power.

Works Consulted

Books

Bruce A. Ackerman and William T. Hassler, *Clean Coal/Dirty Air.* New Haven, CT: Yale University Press, 1981.

Subhankar Banerjee, ed., *Arctic National Wildlife Refuge: Seasons of Life and Land.* Seattle, WA: Mountaineers Books, 2003.

Robert L. Bradley Jr., *Oil, Gas, & Government: The U.S. Experience.* Lanham, MD: Rowman & Littlefield, 1996.

Matthew Brown, "Banking on Disaster: The World Bank and Environmental Destruction," in Donald R. Leal and Roger E. Meiners, eds., *Government vs. Environment.* Lanham, MD: Rowman & Littlefield, 2002.

Edward S. Cassedy, *Prospects for Sustainable Energy: A Critical Assessment.* Cambridge, UK: Cambridge University Press, 2000.

Daniel D. Chiras, *Environmental Science: Creating a Sustainable Future.* Sudbury, MA: Jones and Bartlett, 2001.

David Howard Davis, *Energy Politics.* New York: St. Martin's, 1974.

Paul R. Ehrlich and Anne H. Ehrlich, *Healing the Planet.* Boston, MA: Addison-Wesley, 1991.

————, *Population, Resources, Environment: Issues in Human Ecology.* San Francisco: W.H. Freeman, 1970.

Howard Geller, *Energy Revolution: Policies for a Sustainable Future.* Washington, DC: Island Press, 2003.

Indur M. Goklany, *Clearing the Air: The Real Story of the War on Air Pollution.* Washington, DC: Cato Institute, 1999.

Denis Hayes, *Rays of Hope.* New York: W.W. Norton, 1977.

Jack M. Hollander, *The Real Environmental Crisis.* Berkeley: University of California Press, 2003.

Gary D. Libecap, "Agricultural Programs with Dubious Environmental Benefits: The Political Economy of Ethanol," in Roger E. Meiners and Bruce Yandle, eds., *Agricultural Policy and the Environment.* Lanham, MD: Rowman & Littlefield, 2003.

Bjørn Lomborg, *The Skeptical Environmentalist: Measuring the Real State of the World.* New York: Cambridge University Press, 2001.

S. Charles Maurice and Charles W. Smithson, *The Doomsday Myth: 10,000 Years of Economic Crises.* Stanford, CA: Hoover Institution Press, 1984.

Donella H. Meadows et al., *The Limits to Growth: A Report for the Club of Rome's Project on the Predicament of Mankind.* New York: Universe Books, 1972.

Richard F. Mould, *Chernobyl: The Real Story.* New York: Pergamon, 1988.

F.D. Ommanney, *Lost Leviathan.* New York: Dodd, Mead, 1971.

Jeremy Rifkin, *The Hydrogen Economy: The Creation of the World-Wide Energy Web and the Redistribution of Power on Earth.* New York: Penguin Putnam, 2002.

Julian L. Simon, ed., *The State of Humanity.* Cambridge, MA: Blackwell, 1995.

Robert Stobaugh and Daniel Yergin, eds., *Energy Future.* New York: Random House, 1979.

Jerry Taylor and Peter VanDoren, "Soft Energy Versus Hard Facts: Powering the Twenty-First Century," in Ronald Bailey, ed., *Earth Report 2000.* New York: McGraw-Hill, 2000.

Joe C. Truett and Stephen R. Johnson, eds., *The Natural History of an Arctic Oil Field.* San Diego: Academic Press, 2000.

Periodicals and Short Papers

American Oil & Gas Reporter, "Analyst Predicts Higher Oil, Gas Prices," August 2003.

Dan Balz, "Kerry to Unveil Energy Independence Policy," *Washington Post,* June 13, 2003.

Peter Behr, "U.S. Seeks Hydrogen Fuel Partnership," *Washington Post,* June 16, 2003.

Robert L. Bradley Jr., "The Increasing Sustainability of Conventional Energy," Cato Policy Analysis No. 341, Cato Institute, April 22, 1999.

H. Sterling Burnett, "CAFE's Three Strikes—It Should Be Out," Brief Analysis No. 388, National Center for Policy Analysis, February 13, 2002.

Edward H. Crane and Carl Pope, "Fueled by Pork," *Washington Post,* July 30, 2002.

John Flicker, "Don't Desecrate the Artic Refuge," *Wall Street Journal,* September 18, 1995.

Holly Lippke Fretwell, "Federal Estate: Is Bigger Better?" Public Lands Report III, Political Economy Research Center (PERC), 2000.

Robert Gehrke, "White House Wants to Speed Oil, Gas Drilling," *Bozeman Daily Chronicle,* August 10, 2003.

Steven F. Hayward with Ryan Stowers, "2003 Index of Environmental Indicators," Pacific Research Institute, April 2003.

Deborah Jacobs, "The Caribou and Alaskan Oil," *PERC Reports,* Political Economy Research Center, June 2001.

Tom Kenworthy, "Study Condemns Arctic Oil Drilling," *Washington Post,* August 27, 1995.

Tom Knudson, "State of Denial: A Special Report on the Environment," *Sacramento Bee,* April 27, 2003.

Clay J. Landry, "The Wrong Way to Restore Salmon," *PERC Reports,* Political Economy Research Center, June 2003.

Reid Lea, "A Free Market Environmentalist Discovers He Is One," *PERC Reports,* Political Economy Research Center, August 1992.

Stuart Leuthner, "The Windmills That Won the West," *Invention & Technology,* Fall 2003.

James E. Mielke, "Oil in the Ocean: The Short- and Long-Term Impacts of a Spill," Congressional Research Service Report No. 90-356 SPR, Library of Congress, July 24, 1990.

Nature, "Welcome to the Anthropocene," August 14, 2003.

John U. Nef, "An Early Energy Crisis and Its Consequences," *Scientific American,* November 1977.

Robert H. Nelson, "A Frigid Eden," *Forbes,* April 24, 1995.

Newsweek, "Oil Prices Hit the Skids," January 24, 1983.

————, "Running Out of Everything," November 19, 1973.

Linda Platts, "Garbage to Oil," *PERC Reports,* Political Economy Research Center, June 2003.

John Pomfret, "China's Monumental Gamble," *Washington Post,* June 2, 2003.

Jane Bryant Quinn, "Solar Energy: Mostly Cloudy," *Newsweek,* April 23, 1979.

Robert Rose and Bob Dinneen, "Secondhand Smear," *Washington Post,* June 14, 2003.

Joel Schwartz, "Clearing the Air," *Regulation,* Summer 2003.

Katharine Q. Seelye, "Windmills Sow Dissent for Environmentalists," *New York Times,* June 5, 2003.

Merrill Sheils, "Nuclear Accident," *Newsweek,* April 9, 1979.

Max Singer, "Saudi Arabia's Overrated Oil Weapon," *Weekly Standard,* August 18, 2003.

Vernon L. Smith and Lynne Kiesling, "Demand, Not Supply," *Wall Street Journal,* August 20, 2003.

Allanna Sullivan, "Fates of Alaska Tribes May Ride on Impact of Drilling in Refuge," *Wall Street Journal,* November 2, 1995.

James M. Taylor, "Time to Fight the CAFE Leviathan," *Environment & Climate News,* March 1, 2002.

United States General Accounting Office, "Opportunities to Improve the Management and Oversight of Oil and Gas on Federal Lands," GA0-03-517, August 2003.

Susan Warren and Melanie Trottman, "Getting Unplugged Sheds Light on What Is Wired These Days," *Wall Street Journal,* August 18, 2003.

Dennis A. Williams et al., "Beyond 'The China Syndrome,'" *Newsweek,* April 16, 1979.

Internet Sources

American Wind Energy Association, "The Most Frequently Asked Questions About Wind Energy," May 2002. www.awea.org.

Arctic Power, "Background." www.anwr.org.

Arctic Refuge Science Letter Signatories, letter to President George W. Bush, March 20, 2001. www.defenders.org.

George W. Bush, "Remarks by the President to Capital City Partnership," White House: News, May 17, 2001. www.white house.gov.

———, "State of the Union," White House: News, January 28, 2003. www.whitehouse.gov.

Dan Cahan, "What Is a Fuel Cell?" www.princeton.edu/~dca han/fuelcells/index.shtml.

Defenders of Wildlife, cartoon video. www.savearcticrefuge.org.

———, "Save the Arctic Refuge from Big Oil." www.savearctic refuge.org.

Energy Efficiency and Renewable Energy Network (EERE), "Geothermal Energy Program." www.eere.energy.gov.

Energy Information Administration, *International Energy Annual,* 2001. www.eia.doe.gov.

Environmental Working Group, "Sources of Electricity," 2003. www.ewg.org.

James E. Hansen et al., "Global Warming in the 21st Century: An Alternative Scenario," NASA Goddard Institute for Space Studies, April 17, 2001. www.giss.nasa.gov.

Lynne Kiesling, "The Solution, Not the Problem," Reason Public Policy Institute, August 18, 2003. www.rppi.org.

Benjamin P. Nageak, "Inupiat Eskimos First, Best Environmentalists," Energy Stewardship Alliance, June 30, 2003. www.anwr.org.

Office of Response and Restoration, "The *Exxon Valdez* Oil Spill," National Oceanic and Atmospheric Administration. http://response.restoration.noaa.gov.

Carl Pope, "Sierra Club Urges Balanced Approach That's Quicker, Cleaner, Cheaper, Safer," Sierra Club, June 30, 2003. www.sierraclub.org.

Todd S. Purdum, "California Power Crisis Replays a Familiar Theme," *New York Times,* January 25, 2001. www.nytimes.com.

Jack Raso, "Three Mile Island: A 20th Anniversary Remembrance," American Council on Health and Science, March 1999. www. acsh.org.

Matt Richtel, "Coping Without Electricity in California E–World," *New York Times,* January 28, 2001. www.nytimes.com.

Sea Solar Power International, "The OTEC Technology." www.sea solarpower.com.

Solar Electric Power Association, "Solar Power Basics." www.solar electricpower.org.

Solar PACES, CSP Technologies, "How It Works." www.solar paces.org.

Three Mile Island Alert, "It Was the First Step in a Nuclear Nightmare." www.tmia.com.

Benjamin Zycher, "OPEC," *Concise Encyclopedia of Economics,* Library of Economics and Liberty, 2003. www.econlib.org.

Others

Alan Greenspan, testimony before the U.S. Senate Committee on Energy and Natural Resources, July10, 2003.

Jack Lentfer, written testimony for House Committee on Resources Hearing on Republican Energy Bill "Energy Security Act," July 11, 2001.

"Levelized Costs for Plants by Initial Operation Date [2001 Mills/ k Wh]," spreadsheet e-mailed to author from Jonathan Cogan, Energy Information Administration.

President's Commission on the Accident at TMI, *Report.* Washington, DC: President's Commission, October 1979.

Acknowledgments

Critical Thinking about Environmental Issues: Energy is part of a series designed to bring objectivity to current environmental issues. The authors appreciate the support of two people who recognize the value of treating issues in a fair, balanced, and thorough way. They are Fred L. Smith Jr., president of the Competitive Enterprise Institute in Washington, D.C., and Terry L. Anderson, executive director of PERC—the Center for Free Market Environmentalism—in Bozeman, Montana. We also thank Michael Sanera for his role in initiating this series and are grateful to the Grover Hermann Foundation and the Bass Foundation for their support. We have also benefited from the help of PERC's Michelle Johnson and Michelle McReynolds.

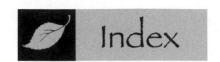 Index

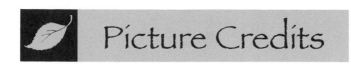

Picture Credits

Cover Credit: The Image Bank

© AFP/CORBIS, 50, 68

© Bettmann/CORBIS, 12, 14, 38, 48

HAYDEN ROGER CELESTIN/EPA/Landov, 81

PETER FORSTER/DPA/Landov, 55

© Colin Garratt; Milepost 92½/CORBIS, 21

© Todd A. Gipstein/CORBIS, 63

FRED GREAVES/Reuters/Landov, 79

Hulton/Archive by Getty Images, 25

© Kim Kulish/CORBIS, 84

ADREES LATIF/Reuters/Landov, 65

JOE MARQUETTE/EPA/Landov, 33

© Charles Mauzy/CORBIS, 27

© DA SILVA PETER/CORBIS, 70

Photodisc, 58, 61

© Richard Michael Pruitt/Dallas Morning News/CORBIS, 75

© Underwood & Underwood/CORBIS, 19

© Kennan Ward/CORBIS, 30

© Nevada Wier/CORBIS, 35

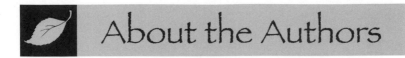# About the Authors

Jane S. Shaw is a senior associate of PERC—the Center for Free Market Environmentalism—in Bozeman, Montana, an institute dedicated to improving environmental quality through markets. Shaw is the author of *Global Warming,* one of the books in the Critical Thinking About Environmental Issues series, and coauthor with Michael Sanera of *Facts, Not Fear: Teaching Children About the Environment.* Before joining PERC, Shaw was an associate economics editor of *Business Week* magazine.

Manuel Nikel-Zueger received a bachelor's degree in economics from the University of Arizona and became a research associate with PERC, where he studied economic and environmental issues. He is skilled in horsemanship, spent a summer fishing and processing salmon commercially, and has interned at a U.S. senator's office.